HALLS OF FAME

OF

MY BOOK HOUSE

EDITED BY

OLIVE BEAUPRÉ MILLER

PUBLISHERS

THE BOOK HOUSE for CHILDREN

CHICAGO

PRINTED IN U.S.A.

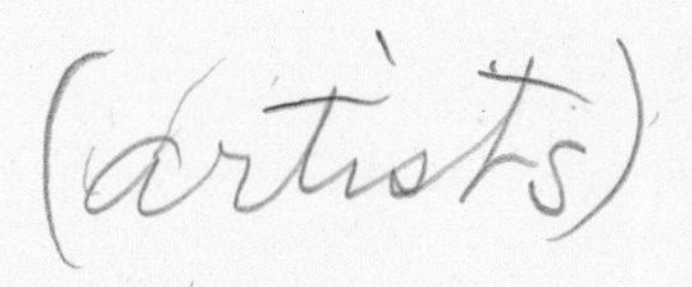

CONTENTS

CHILDHOOD BIOGRAPHIES OF AUTHORS

CHILDHOOD BIOGRAPHIES OF AUTHORS (*continued*)

The Royal Page

GEOFFREY CHAUCER (*English*, 1340-1400)

IN days when all the great people of England were Norman-French and the poor people were Anglo-Saxons, a swine-herd met a cow-herd and a sheep-herd on a green sweep of rolling meadow beyond which rose the gray towers of ancient castle walls.

"All the good things in the land be for the Norman-French since the days when William the Norman conquered our Saxon England," said the swine-herd, pointing to the castle. "When these beasts of ours be out here in the meadow and a poor man must work to tend them, how do you call them, friend?"

"Why, man, I call them *swine*," the cow-herd answered thickly.

"And *swine* is Anglo-Saxon—good Anglo-Saxon," the swine-herd nodded with emphasis, "but how call you that same beast when he is served up at table before lordly ladies and gentlemen?"

"Why, then I call him *pork*."

Read *The Chaucer Story Book*, by Eva M. Tappan, and *The Canterbury Pilgrims*, by F. J. H. Darton.

"And *pork* is Norman-French!" The swine-herd continued to grumble. "The beast is Saxon when a poor man by the sweat of his brow must tend him, but French when lords and ladies may take their pleasure of him! And you, friend cow-herd, your *cow* and likewise your *ox* are Saxon. They're lowly Saxon beasts when you tend them in the field, but look you, they change, as by magic, to lordly French *beef* at table!"

"Aye," interrupted the sheep-herd. "The very word *pleasure* is French but *work* is Anglo-Saxon! Right you are, friend swine-herd. Even the language we speak since the days of William the Conqueror shows all the good things of life be for the Norman-French. Whatever is noble and courtly and giveth joy and pleasure, that must have a French name, but for everything lowly and homely there must be a Saxon word!" The cow-herd, the swine-herd and the sheep-herd solemnly shook their heads.

Now in these days there dwelt at the court of King Edward the Third of England a young page named Geoffrey Chaucer. Clad in red and black breeches, with a short cloak and elegant shoes, he attended upon his mistress, the wife of King Edward's son, at many a gay festivity. Often in some chamber with beautiful tapestried walls he sat amid lords and ladies while someone read a poem to entertain the party and though it was three hundred years since William the Norman had come with a mighty army from France and conquered the Saxon King Harold in the bloody battle of Hastings, the poems read in these chambers were always written in French. Who would use Saxon English, the language of churls and peasants? True, the common people of England already spoke a mixture of Anglo-Saxon and French, but their common English was vulgar, the tongue of the man in the streets! It was rude. It was not for nobles. In the court one must speak only French. Ere long young Geoffrey himself began to write poems in French, in the slight, graceful, shallow manner of the poets across the water.

Living like any young page, Geoffrey was barely nineteen, when he went with the King to France to fight England's battles there. In the stress and struggle and bloodshed he bore himself right nobly till the days of the English retreat. Then he was taken captive and for months he languished in prison. But King Edward held him so dear that he paid a ransom to free him. Thereafter, behold young Geoffrey again returned to England and in the King's own household, risen to be a squire with an annual salary and a gift of handsome clothes at every Christmastide. Soon there were wedding bells and Geoffrey was taking a bride, the beautiful young Philippa, a lady-in-waiting to the Queen.

As years went by, his master sent him on important missions to many a foreign port, to Genoa, to France, to Flanders. A deal of the world Geoffrey Chaucer saw on his travels for the King! In Italy he was touched by the warm, glowing charm of the land and by the rich depth and color of Italy's powerful writers, Dante, Petrarch and Boccaccio. Now he could no more be satisfied with the poems he wrote in French. They might be graceful and tender, but they were slight and shallow. Henceforth he wished to write with all the depth and fire of the great Italian poets.

As a new departure in time he devoted himself to business. Being made Comptroller of Customs at the busy port of London, he spent his days at the wharves, recording trade in wool and hides, talking with stevedores and sea-going men and seeing human nature of quite a different sort from that he had known at court. He began to know the common man and to hear almost altogether the language he spoke, the vulgar tongue of the English.

A courtier, a poet, a diplomat, a man of business was Chaucer, ever active in many affairs. In 1386, at the very height of his glory, he sat in Parliament as a Knight of the Shire from Kent. But thereafter misfortunes befell him. He lost all his friends at court; his offices were taken from him and he was obliged henceforth to live among common people with a purse exceedingly lean.

But now what new life for his poetry! At last he wrote no more after the French or Italian fashion. He was out of life at the court. He was living with the common man. For him he would write in English. He would use the despised English tongue! Save for the poems of a ploughman or some such man of the people, English had heretofore never been used in literature. But Chaucer now burst forth with beautiful poems in English, vivacious, full of humor, tender and delighting in nature, singing of all the "smale foweles" that "maken melodye," of sunshine and soft breezes, of April's fresh, sweet showers. His greatest work was *Canterbury Tales*, a rich and colorful picture of Old England in those days. Down along the white and dusty Kentish road, a company of pilgrims wended their way on horseback, journeying to the shrine of St. Thomas Becket at Canterbury. From every walk of life they came, — knight, squire, miller, monk, doctor, merchant, churl; and as they journeyed they told the stories Chaucer related, now one all courtliness of phrase, now one overflowing with the broad coarse humor of the churl.

Thus it was that Chaucer made the homely English tongue the language of a new and splendid literature which was to follow him through the years. This was the great thing he did. English literature really began with Geoffrey Chaucer.

In the Sixth Century, Anglo-Saxon invaders drove the original Britons, who spoke Celtic, into Wales, Cornwall, and the Scottish Highlands. Their Saxon England ended with the Norman Conquest, 1066. Gradually English became a mixture of Anglo-Saxon and Norman-French with some remaining Celtic words. See pages 22, 44, Vol. I. Tales of King Arthur are Celtic. Saxon poems by Caedmon 665, A.D.; works of the Venerable Bede; *Beowulf*, the oldest English epic; the Anglo-Saxon *Chronicle*, systematized by King Alfred; *The Vision of Piers the Ploughman;* and Wyclif's translation of *The Bible* constitute the literature of Saxon-England before Chaucer. The first English printing, by William Caxton, 1475, made books more widely read. He printed *Canterbury Tales*.

Down by the River Avon

WILLIAM SHAKESPEARE (*English*, 1564-1616)

BEYOND Sir Hugh Clopton's noble old stone bridge that spans the Avon with fourteen splendid arches, rise the quaint gables and cathedral spire of Stratford town. In the days of good Queen Bess the houses were ancient plaster buildings crossed with timber and each had at the sides or rear a gay little garden, bright with flowers. In one of the best of those houses on Henley Street lived Master Will Shakespeare, a high spirited lad with a fine, courtly bearing and pleasant hazel eyes. His father, John Shakespeare, once High Bailiff or Mayor of Stratford, was a well-to-do merchant, a trader in hides, leather-goods, wool, meats, and goodness knows what besides. His mother, Mary Arden, was a blithe and womanly matron, who shed a warmth of tenderness through the merry, little home circle.

Over in the old, old grammar school, with its jutting second story abutting on the street, Master Will and the other Stratford urchins learned their lessons. There they conned arithmetic, a bit of Latin and Greek, and the precepts of good manners, from six o'clock in the morning till five-thirty in the evening,

Read *Master Skylark*, a story of Shakespeare's time, by John Bennett; *Will Shakespeare's Little Lad*, by Imogene Clark; and *Tales from Shakespeare*, by Charles and Mary Lamb.

and the schoolmaster sitting over them was all too well versed in the use of the birchen rod.

But it was a gay and joyous life, in spite of lessons, that they led in Stratford town. Warwickshire in those days was divided into two well marked divisions by the river Avon. To the south lay the rich green pasture land of Feldon, stretching away to the blue line of the distant Cotswold hills, and dotted here and there by herds of cattle and flocks of snow-white sheep. Amid little clumps of protecting elms nestled cozy homesteads, and past the well tilled fields flowed placid rivers, their limpid waters overhung by alders and silverwillows. To the north of the Avon, however—Ah! there was no cultivated land, but the wild, free forest of Arden, sweeping out over hill and dale for twenty miles, the delight of all boyish hearts. When school time was over, then for Will Shakespeare and the other Stratford boys, it was Heigh the doxy over the dale! We're off for the Forest of Arden!

O, the sweetness of those woodland haunts, the exhilaration and breadth and joy! The boys raced through leafy covert and sunny glade, past giant oaks and tangled thickets, now skipping from stone to stone across the brawling brooks, now cleaving the woodland stillness with their shrill young voices. Sometimes a dappled herd of deer swept away before them across an open lawn or twinkled through the leaves amid the shadowy bracken, while groups of timid rabbits fed here and there on the tender leaves. In the air was the melody of birds, the warble of wren and throstle. Will Shakespeare talked with every keeper and woodsman in the forest till he knew intimately all the ins and outs of that glorious sylvan life and could carol a tirra-lirra with the merriest of the larks.

At times, too, young Will wandered through the picturesque towns and little forest villages round about, past the old gray castles and abbeys that loomed within their parks shut off by palings from the wilderness of Arden. Some of these castles had been abandoned and dismantled during the Wars of the Roses. Silent now as the surrounding forest they stood, half ruined, and haunted with shadowy memories of lords and ladies and all the stately revelry that had once held sway within their walls. It was a country full of interest, full of history, full of stirring border legends of the days when the English stood sturdily against the insurgents of Wales. Every hill and stream, every grim old abbey and castle had its heroic tale of long ago.

On market days and fair days there was great excitement in the town itself for Master Will, for Stratford was the center of a famous agricultural and grazing district. On a bright summer's day, Will would rise with the sun and make off from Henley Street to see the countrywomen come in, jogging along on horseback, their panniers laden with chickens, butter and eggs, or to watch the droves of slow oxen come crowding over Clopton Bridge, and the herds of Herefordshire cows, lowing anxiously after their skittish young calves. Then he would follow the cattle to Rother Market, where the cattle dealers gathered about Market Cross, and observe the humors of the ploughman and drovers, scarcely less stolid and deliberate of movement and speech than their oxen.

At the jovial Fair-season, the streets of Stratford were alive with jugglers and minstrels, harpers singing old ballads, and lads and lassies dancing their country measures. At such times it seemed as though the wealth of the world had been dumped into Stratford-town. There in the booths were wheat and wool, cheese and wax, clothes and stout linen napery. Besides all this, there was many a wandering peddler, carrying trinkets and trumpery such as country swains buy for their sweethearts—ribbons and gloves, masks and coifs, stomachers and bracelets.

Not far from Stratford lay the little forest village of Snitterfield, where Will's grandfather and Uncle Henry Shakespeare had their farms. Every boundary tree and stone, every pond and sheep-pool, every barn and cattleshed on the way to his Uncle Henry's farm, Will knew by heart, for he dearly loved the place and spent many a happy day there. At Snitterfield Will trotted around after his uncle, poking with eager interest into all the byres and barns and poultry yards. Now and again, from a safe nook on the bushy margin of a pool, he enjoyed the fun and excitement of the sheep washing, or watched the mysteries of the sheep shearing. Then he would remain to the shearing feast, eat the cheese-cakes and warden-pies, and see the young maid who was chosen Queen of the Festival receive her rustic guests and distribute among them her gifts of flowers. Indeed, Will Shakespeare's youth was passed amid the labors and pastimes, the recurring festivals and varying round of a rural community. Each incident of the year, seedtime and harvest, summer and winter, brought its own group of picturesque merry-makings in those forest farms and villages.

The best loved holiday of all was May-day, a spontaneous outburst of joy, a gladsome welcome to the re-awakening life and freshness of the spring. Very early in the morning, before dawn, lads and lassies went out into the woods and brought back branches of trees and garlands of flowers to build leafy bowers and arbors in the streets of the city. Then, with twenty sleek yoke of oxen, each one bearing a nosegay of blossoms on his horns, they dragged home the Maypole, all bound around with flowers. When the May-pole was reared in the center of the city with streamers and banners flying, men, women and children fell to dancing and feasting about it.

Hey ding-a-ding! Sweet lovers love the spring!

On May-day there were the Morris dancers, dancing their jovial measures, and masquerading

as Robin Hood, Friar Tuck and Little John. And there was Maid Marian, Queen of the May, and the Fool in his motley dress with cap and bells. There was the Hobby Horse performing ridiculous antics and the comical, waddling dragon, and jolly Tom Piper, the musician of the troop. It was well that May-day was a holiday in the Stratford schools, so that Master Will Shakespeare did not have to play truant to witness such scenes as these.

Christmas was merry, too, though it had a deeper note as well befitted the season. The great Yule log, like the Maypole, was dragged in with shouts and music and joyously laid on the hearth. On Christmas Eve, the waits, their noses red from cold, went round from door to door through the snow, singing their carols and hymns,—"As Joseph was a-walking, he heard an angel sing."

The great cross of Stratford was garnished with holly, ivy and bay, and in every household hospitality reigned. The manor house of the Cloptons among the trees overlooking the town, was a-bustle with preparations, its chimneys belching smoke, the sounds of pipe and trumpet issuing from its doors. Long tables were spread for the guests; the master and mistress took their seats at the head of the board with their friends and principal tenants about them; the Boar's head was brought in with solemn ceremony, and the Lord of Misrule with his jovial attendants became the master of the feast. Thereafter was dancing till curfew, then home through the moonlight to Stratford.

So went the joyous round of life in Stratford-town and each recurring holiday brought its own particular mumming and masking and playing of parts, but there were real players, too, sometimes to be seen in the city.

The very oldest form of play loved by the people in England was the miracle or mystery play, presenting some tale from the Bible. At first, long years before Shakespeare's time, these plays had been given in the churches by the clergy, but gradually they had moved out to the church yard. Then the actors had changed from the clergy to citizens, members of the various trade guilds of the towns. Later still they were presented on a pageant cart, which was moved about from place to place, and gave a performance wherever it stopped. The actors would play the story of Noah's flood, or Adam and Eve, or indeed any tale from Creation to the Last Judgment.

These carts had two stories, an upper one for the stage, and a lower one which was curtained to provide a dressing room for the actors. Over all was a canopy of carved and gilded woodwork cut into battlements and a-flutter with bright-colored banners. Usually men dragged these carts through the streets, but at times they were drawn by horses, and their approach was heralded by jesters and tumblers who ran along before them.

The action of the play took place on the upper platform, but sometimes the actors stepped down into the street, particularly if they wished to present such a scene as the grim and gaping jaws of Hell. This Hell-mouth was the most elaborate and costly theatrical property owned by the trade guilds. It was used in several plays but especially in the Last Judgment,—a huge and grotesque head of canvas with a vast gaping mouth armed with fangs. The jaws were made to open and shut, a light within gave the effect of flames, and whenever the devil carried off a lost soul, there was a great noise in the beast's interior made by the rattling of pans and kettles, while thick smoke issued from his mouth. The making and repairing of this Hell-mouth was a constant expense to the trade guilds, and frequent entries like the following appear in their books of accounts:

Paid for making and painting Hell-mouth..........12 pence
Paid for keeping of fire at Hell-mouth............. 4 pence

Lost souls were dressed in black or yellow to represent flames, saved souls were robed in white. The Devil wore a grizzly mask, was shaggy and beast-like, with horns, cloven feet, and forked tail, and he carried a club with which he laid about him vigorously. He was attended by a company of little demons, their coats covered with horsehair to make them look like awesome monsters. Vice was likewise a constant attendant on the Devil, but he gradually became no more than a mere buffoon or clown to set the crowd a-laughing. Indeed, the plays themselves in time acquired parts that were all too hilarious. Noah's wife

became a comic character, a shrew who laid about her with a cutting tongue and sent the audience into an uproar before she could be dragged off into the ark.

The representative of Jesus wore a gilt wig and a coat of white leather, painted and gilded. King Herod, who was a very important character and blustered about the stage in a manner that became proverbial, was dressed like a Turk and bore a sword and helmet. Herod and Pilate, Cain and Judas, Turks and infidels, as well as the Devil, were favorite characters of these mysteries.

In time, however, morality plays became even more popular than the mysteries. In the moralities, Bible stories were no longer presented, but all manner of Vices and all manner of Virtues were portrayed as persons who did battle with each other in order to gain possession of man's soul. It was some such performances as these that Will Shakespeare used to see as a boy, though in his day it was customary to draw the pageant cart up in the courtyard of some inn, rather than to leave it in the street. The common people then crowded around it, standing, while the richer ones paid a large fee to have seats in the balconies or windows of the inn that overlooked the yard.

Coventry, a town near Stratford, was one of the chief centers for the production of miracle plays, and Shakespeare must certainly have gone over there at times to see them. Moreover, the various trade guilds, plasterers, tanners, armourers, hosiers, etc., who presented the plays, were in the habit of visiting neighboring cities, and doubtless performed in Stratford.

When Will was only five years old, his father, then Mayor of Stratford, especially invited to the city some of the real stage players, who made a business of acting and were beginning to replace the old performers of the guilds. Later, the best companies in the kingdom came to Stratford, including the Earl of Leicester's Company from London. So young Will had plenty of opportunity to study the making and presenting of plays, to acquire a deep love for the theatre, and perhaps sometimes even to act himself and make friends with the strolling players.

But now when Will was still little more than a boy, his father began to have business failures and his affairs to go down, down, down in the world. Soon it became necessary for the lad to be taken from school and put to work to help out in his father's business. John Shakespeare had been imprudently extravagant in his prosperity, and now he lost his grip and let himself sink beneath misfortune. He would not go to church, he would not see his friends, he would not show himself at any public meeting. Sweet Mary Arden, however, bore up nobly under their troubles, her spirit as calm and serene in the dark days as it had been in the bright. How the boy loved and admired his mother! All his life long she lived in his heart as the very embodiment of every womanly virtue.

Will sympathized ardently with his parents in their troubles, and was willing to do any kind of work to help them. Moreover, those very troubles awakened his independence and taught him to be scrupulously honorable in his own business dealings with others, a trait which he never forgot. An open, frank, generous young fellow was Will Shakespeare in those days, innately courteous and wholly lovable.

When Will was only eighteen, he was many a day to be seen making off across the fields, with daisies pied, to the little hamlet of Shottery, which lay half concealed by aged elms, its cozy homesteads nestling amid blossoming fruit-trees and brilliant gardens. Here in a lovely old cottage, with a quaint thatched roof, lived Anne Hathaway, the daughter of a friend of Will's father, a maid whom he had known all his life. In the garden and through the primrose lanes the two lingered often together, and soon there was news of their wedding.

Boy that he was, Will was only nineteen when his first daughter, Suzanne, was born. Now what was there to do? He had a family on his hands to support and his father's business grew every day worse and worse. Two years later twins were born to him, a boy and a girl, Hamnet and Judith, and then an event occurred which made the young man decide that the only thing for him to do was to be off to London and seek his fortunes there.

He was out hunting one day with some comrades when they pursued a fine deer into Fullbroke Park, or perhaps across the shallow ford of the river to Charlecote Park. Now Charlecote Park was the property of a sour and gloomy old Puritan, Sir Thomas Lucy, a man of aristocratic pride and narrowness who hated all youthful frolics and merriment. Just as they had killed the buck, the youths fell in with one of Sir Thomas's keepers, who insisted violently that they had no right to hunt where they were and accused them of being deer-stealers. Master Will defended himself right spiritedly against the charge, indeed it is even said that he posted certain none too respectful placards on Sir Thomas Lucy's gate. Sir Thomas in high dudgeon complained to the authorities in Stratford. These honorable gentlemen, fearing to offend so rich and powerful a man, doubtless let it be known to Will that it would be better for him to leave town for a time. Accordingly, behold young Will, bidding his wife and babes farewell and off for London town.

It was about 1585 or 1587 when Will Shakespeare arrived in London. In those days players were just beginning to be recognized as respectable folk. Heretofore, they had been looked down upon as wandering, beggarly fellows. Certain writers of education,

such as Greene and Peele and Marlowe, had been among the first to think the writing of plays a vocation worthy of their dignity, and were turning out dramas vastly more like our modern ones than the old moralities and mysteries. Ten years before, Queen Elizabeth had given the Earl of Leicester's players the first legal permit to act in certain places in London, and James Burbage, the leader of these players, had built *The Theatre* at Shoreditch, just outside the boundaries of the city, for mayor and common council still frowned darkly on the presentation of plays within the sacred precincts of the town.

In building his theatre, Burbage took his plan from the old courtyards of the inns where it had been customary to draw up the pageant carts. The square yard where poorer people stood, became the pit of the theatre, the pageant cart the stage, the balconies whence the wealthier class had looked on, the gallery or boxes. The stage and galleries were the only part of the building covered, which was none too comfortable for the people in the pit if a sudden storm came pelting down.

It was at *The Theatre* that Master Will first found occupation by holding the horses of the gaily dressed young gallants who attended the performances. There he stood before the door in all kinds of weather, with Hey, ho, the wind and the rain! But he soon advanced from this work to acting. Then he began to write over faulty old plays, and at last he took to writing splendid new dramas of his own. In a very short time he had surpassed all the dramatists of his day and held the foremost place in the hearts of the playgoing public.

Before Shakespeare's plays were produced, the merry farces *Ralph Roister Doister*, by Nicholas Udall, and *Gammer Gurton's Needle*, by William Stevenson, had been entertaining the English public. The plays of Greene and Peele, of Christopher Marlowe and the "rare Ben Jonson" were written in the days of Shakespeare.

Many a time in those days, however, amid the noise and babble of London, there flashed upon his inward eye, quiet pictures of willows "growing aslant a brook," of orchards when "the moon tips with silver all the fruit tree tops." Many a time he thought of the blue-veined violets, the cowslips and ladies-smocks that grew in the meadows by the Avon. He heard again the "throstle with his note so true, the wren with little quill," and the very notes of those songsters warbled their way into the music of his words. Indeed, he carried the meadows of the Avon, the forest of Arden, the sunburnt sicklemen and merry maidens of his homeland with him to London, and these came forever glancing out here and there in his plays. Aye, his home on the Avon was the beacon that loomed ever before him, beckoning, and the craving always lived in his heart for his beautiful native heath.

But, withal, young Will kept his head marvelously well in spite of his success, and he avoided the wild dissipations that were ruining his fellow-dramatists, though he loved life and mirth as well as any and had no smallest trace of harshness in

his blithe and genial nature. He worked hard, studying at French and Italian in his spare time, saving money for his family and making visits every year to his beloved Stratford.

He was first a member of the Earl of Leicester's players which later became the Lord Chamberlain's Company and the favorite company of the Queen. All the players in London in those days, save for certain bands of children, were divided into two companies, the Lord Admiral's and the Lord Chamberlain's, and many a time they went to perform before Queen Bess herself.

The theatres where Shakespeare's plays were given were *The Globe* erected outside the city, and *Blackfriar's* which was practically in the town. The actors played at *The Globe* in summer and at *Blackfriar's* in the winter. *Blackfriar's* was completely roofed in and lit by torchlight so performances could be given there in the evening, but at *The Globe* the pit was uncovered and performances were only given by day.

The common people had a merry time standing in the pit, munching apples and nuts, jostling and chaffing good-naturedly under the open sky, while the fine ladies and gentlemen, who did not wish to mingle with these "groundlings," had their own boxes in the covered balconies, the ladies occupying the seats, the gentlemen reclining at their feet. If they chose, they played cards during the performance and there were always pages ready to attend upon their needs. Whoever paid extra could sit upon the stage itself. There was no scenery on that stage and a simple printed placard announced the name of the place where the scene was supposed to be laid. Women's parts were taken by men. It was not until long after Shakespeare's time that women appeared on the stage. The hoisting of a flag and the blowing of a trumpet bade all be still to hear the play.

What an age of awakened national life and stirring spirit was that of good Queen Bess, when the minds of men had burst the bonds of the Dark Ages and were eagerly inquiring and adventuring everywhere. Along the river side and in noble houses on the Strand were the hardy mariners and adventurous sea captains, Drake, Hawkins and Frobisher, who had driven their dauntless keels fearlessly into the unknown seas of the new world, in order to push back the limits of man's knowledge. The greater number of eager and excited listeners who crowded the rude theatres from floor to roof had shared the adventurous exploits of the age and felt the keenest interest in life and vivid action. So the drama of the day became the mirror in which all these active forces were reflected.

But, besides the Americas, there was another new world which men were most anxious to explore in that age of awakened inquiry, that is, the world of human nature, heretofore left so little questioned and understood. All the traits and impulses of that nature, good and bad, its high hopes and aspirations, its fears and sorrows, its bigness and its littleness,—there was need of a map to point them all out. Into that unknown sea sailed the intrepid mariner, Shakespeare, and he charted it in his mighty dramas as none other has ever done, the great Columbus of the newly discovered world of man's heart and mind and spirit.

For twenty years he worked actively in London, twenty long years, but at last a great wave of home-yearning called him back forever to the primrose lanes of Stratford. He had already bought a fine house there for his family, and here he settled down, to spend his remaining years in peace and quiet, honored and loved by all. No other man ever knew the hearts of men and women as Shakespeare did. He still remains the greatest dramatist of all ages who wrote "not for an age but for all time."

Under the Stuart kings, James I and Charles I, who followed Queen Elizabeth, the vitality and joy of this period found expression in the graceful poems of Robert Herrick and the Cavalier poets, Richard Lovelace and Thomas Carew, courtiers in the reign of Charles I (1625-1649). In sharp contrast to the Cavalier poets was the intense and majestic John Milton with his magnificent *Paradise Lost*. Milton embodied all the Puritan feeling which ruled England under Oliver Cromwell, whose battles with the Cavaliers ended in the beheading of Charles I. Richard Lovelace, cast into prison for his Cavalier sympathies and still blithely singing, "Stone walls do not a prison make nor iron bars a cage," is a noble figure on one side. Opposite him is the dignified stateliness of the blind Milton, dictating *Paradise Lost* to his daughters or pouring forth out of his blindness his longing for the light he had lost in "Hail, holy light!" Milton (1608-1674) was the great figure of the period following Elizabeth.

Kilcolman Castle

EDMUND SPENSER (*English*, 1552-1599)

KILCOLMAN CASTLE in the County of Cork stood on the north side of a fine lake, looking off across a plain to a fringe of wooded uplands, and commanding a view over half the breadth of Ireland. Once it had belonged to the Earl of Desmond, a champion of Irish freedom, but it had been lost to him in a recent rebellion which he had led against the government of England. It lay now a romantic old ruin, scarred and broken with the turbulencies of the past; and mid its shattered walls, as in some sequestered glade, lived one who sang sweetly, piped to the woods, and passed his days in peace and quiet like any shepherd among the flowery meadows.

Edmund Spenser was an English poet to whom the old castle had been given by the government. He had come to Ireland in 1580 as secretary to the Lord Deputy, and there he had remained holding one clerkship after another, dreaming his dreams, and all unconscious of the hatred that was smouldering round about him, like a seething volcano, in the hearts of the Irish people.

It was no small sacrifice to remain away from London in the days of Queen Elizabeth. No more to see Sir Philip Sidney, Spenser's true ideal of knighthood! To be parted from that brilliant young dramatist, William Shakespeare! To hear of the defeat of the Spanish Armada, and the exploits of Drake and Hawkins and Frobisher, only as a distant echo! But Spenser carried his own world with him wherever he went, and he found high company in the very air that flowed around him.

One day his old friend, Sir Walter Raleigh, came along to pay him a visit. Spenser told him that he was writing a poem called

The Faerie Queene. He had finished three books and he meant to write nine more, each one to have as hero a different knight who should represent some one of the principal virtues. Raleigh enthusiastically advised him to take these books to London and he himself presented the poet to the Queen. Now Spenser had already become famous through *The Shepherd's Calendar* which he had published ten years before and the public received his new work with delight and admiration. How sweet was its melody, how abundant its fancy! Queen Elizabeth herself granted the poet a little pension. For two hundred years there had been no great poem written in the English language. *The Faerie Queene* was the first great work since the days of Geoffrey Chaucer.

Nevertheless Spenser was glad to leave London and go back to Kilcolman Castle, and he celebrated his return with a song called *Colin Clout's Come Home Again.* By and by he fell in love with a lady named Elizabeth, and there was a long, long wooing, but at last she answered him aye, and he sang the finest wedding song ever written in English. Beneath the evening star and the fair face of the moon he brought his lady home to be the mistress of his heart. For four happy years he lived with his wife and little children at Kilcolman Castle and the publication of three more books of the *Faerie Queene* raised him to the pinnacle of fame, though they brought him little money. Then alack! the volcano that had slumbered so long burst into eruption. While he had dreamed his dreams in the valley, fierce curses had been uttered against him from the hills around. The peasant folk remembered their Irish lord whom they had been wont to see come in his splendour to Kilcolman, and their souls were filled with hate, for memory of Lord Desmond. Rushing down on Kilcolman they plundered it and set it on fire. The poet, his wife and babies barely escaped the flames. In profound distress they went to London and shortly afterward Spenser died.

Spenser's *Faerie Queene* was dedicated to Queen Elizabeth and many of its characters represented people of that time. Gloriana was Queen Elizabeth, herself. A master of beautiful words joined in musical sequence, Spenser left poems of such lyrical charm and richness of poetical expression that they had great influence on later poets.

In the Days of Queen Anne

JOSEPH ADDISON (1672–1719)
SIR RICHARD STEELE (1672–1729)

IN days when Queen Anne sat on the throne of England, Dick Steele, his eyes agleam with the light of Irish vivacity, walked the streets of London. He dodged among hackney coaches and fashionable sedan chairs. He escaped the persuasive arts of apprentices and shopkeepers, trying to invite him to buy at the sign of the blue boar, the black swan or the hog in armor. He avoided a quarrel with a dandy who seized the inside of the side-walk and pressed close in to the wall to save his fine clothes from the flood that came gushing out of a water-spout and over into the gutter. There went the sauntering fop in embroidered coat and knee-breeches, carrying a little muff to keep his hands from the cold! And there went milady, too, in a fine sedan chair borne by

When Addison was a baby, John Bunyan, imprisoned for non-conformist preaching, wrote *Pilgrim's Progress.*

servants. Now she descended to the ground with a monkey under her arm and minced along down the street in order to see the fashions, her skirts enormously full, her heels enormously high, and her white skin set off with black patches cut into moons and stars.

Dick Steele knew very well the whims of that precious great lady. His own wife, Prue, was a petulant, difficult little piece, requiring plenty of patience. If the weather was gloomy enough, milady would stay at home and have the "vapors," that is, be moody and irritable; she would weep and grow hysterical or possibly manage to faint if crossed in her desires. She did nothing that was useful nor did she indulge in exercise save for dancing through the masked ball, the minuet or the country dance. But Dick Steele saw all these poses and artificialities of people with a very kindly eye. Tender and gallant with his wife, warm-hearted and witty with others, he was a lovable fellow.

In those days a coffee or chocolate house was the proper place for a man to go and meet his acquaintances and Steele was now on his way to meet his friend, Joseph Addison. At the coffee house one would find gathered mid a brilliant flow of conversation all the wits, gallants, politicians, poets and essayists of the age. Perhaps Steele would see the grave old satirist, Jonathan Swift, the author of *Gulliver's Travels*, stalking up and down, glum and silent between the tables, or he might meet the little poet, Alexander Pope, or, better still, as he laid down his penny of admission, he might rub shoulders with a highwayman who, carefully masked, had robbed him the very evening before!

At Button's Coffee House Addison was now the central figure. So charming was his conversation, so delicate his humor, that he was accounted the leader among the wits and writers of the day. From their school-days at Charterhouse, Addison, grave, reserved, but kindly, had been the friend of Dick Steele, the impetuous Irish orphan. They had been at Oxford together and when Steele, returning home from a period of fighting in France, had started a

Swift meant *Gulliver's Travels* as a bitter satire on English life, but children loved the fancies he made so real.

paper called *The Tatler*, Addison had been a contributor. Now in 1711 the two joined forces to publish a famous daily journal called *The Spectator*.

Nine years before, daily papers had been unknown in London. For news people still depended on what they heard at the coffee house or on the queer little news-letter, a journal written out by an editor and copied by hand by his clerks, with half of the sheet left blank so that the buyer might add his own private correspondence before he mailed it to friends. Likewise there were some weeklies, but news in the papers was meager and mixed with contemptible gossip, stars and asterisks being used in place of the names of people. *The Spectator* now appeared as the first real daily paper, though it reported no news and printed no political discussions, being merely a daily essay for people of fashion to read over their morning chocolate.

Addison and Steele had plenty to talk about as they sipped their coffee together. They had set themselves to civilize a lot of English barbarians who already considered themselves the most civilized of men. For people whose sole concern had been oaths, coquetry, duelling or the latest affectation in dress, they meant to set up simple and wholesome ideals of life and to make these standards popular. Creating the interesting character of old Sir Roger de Coverley, a genial country squire supposed to belong to a club of which the Spectator was also a member, they made Sir Roger hold forth in his simple, kindly way on the faults and foibles of his time and thus they jested at extravagance, made vanity ridiculous and held meanness up to contempt.

There was certainly enough that needed correcting in the London of Queen Anne. At night the little street lamps diffused so little light that the city was left in darkness and every man with an honest errand had to engage a torch-bearer to light him on his way. Watchmen cried the hours of the night, and the state of the weather, but they had no wit whatever to serve anyone in danger and dangers there were in plenty. The greatest fear after dark came not from ordinary criminals, though these were common enough, but from bands of aristocratic young rowdies with too little to do and too much money to spend, their funds coming all too easily from great landed estates in the country. The most notorious of these bands was called the Mohocks. They would seize some peaceable citizen, roll him about in a barrel, tattoo his face, perhaps, or imitating the fox hunt, chase him till they had him at their mercy, then keep him dancing with pricks of their swords. Against such abuses as these the editors of *The Spectator* directed their busy pens. They earnestly tried, too, to write better dramas to take the place of the coarse plays people regarded as entertaining. The theatre was the favorite place of meeting. There at six o'clock the fashionable world gathered to see and to be seen.

For over a year Steele and Addison continued *The Spectator Papers*. Later Steele went to Parliament and Addison settled down on a large estate in Warwickshire, having married Lady Warwick. Toward the close of Addison's life a sorry quarrel arose and separated him from Steele, a sad page with which to end the story of their friendship, but *The Spectator Papers* remain a monument to their efforts and a graphic picture of life in the days of Queen Anne.

From Steele's account of Alexander Selkirk's adventures, Defoe wrote *Robinson Crusoe*, in 1714, (Vol. IX, p. 40).

Old Noll

OLIVER GOLDSMITH (*Irish*, 1728-1774)

Nolly Goldsmith, for shortness called Noll,
Who wrote like an angel, but talked like poor Poll!

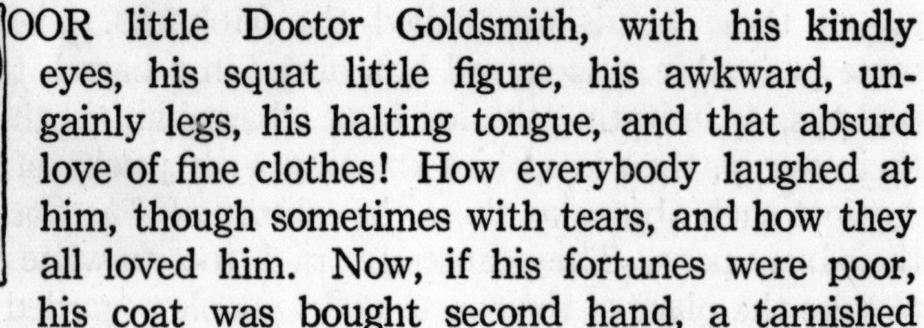

POOR little Doctor Goldsmith, with his kindly eyes, his squat little figure, his awkward, ungainly legs, his halting tongue, and that absurd love of fine clothes! How everybody laughed at him, though sometimes with tears, and how they all loved him. Now, if his fortunes were poor, his coat was bought second hand, a tarnished green and gold with an ugly patch on the breast, but he strutted along quite proudly and carefully hid the patch by holding his hat well over it; now, when his fortunes were fine, he blossomed out in peach-color, claret, sky-blue! And yet, in spite of his vanity and a thousand other weaknesses, what a great, generous, loving heart! Who could do other than love him?

He had always a crowd of children at his heels, had little Doctor Goldsmith. His favorite enjoyment was to romp with them, the merriest and noisiest of all. Sometimes he played them a tune on his flute, sang them an Irish song, or told them stories of Irish fairies. Again, he led them at blindman's buff, or a game of hunt-the-slipper. And if the children were very small, he would turn his wig hindside before and play ridiculous tricks to amuse them.

Once when he was drinking coffee with a friend, he took the friend's little five-year old son up tenderly on his knee. Moved by some perverse instinct, what did the tiny George Coleman do, but slap him on the face, a spiteful rap that left a tingling red mark. The father indignantly took his small son and locked him up alone to suffer for his crime by solitary imprisonment in the dark. But soon, very soon, there was some one come to the little fellow's rescue, some one holding a candle and smiling tenderly.

It was Dr. Goldsmith himself. Georgie sulked and sobbed at first, but Goldsmith fondled and soothed him until he began to brighten. Then the little Doctor placed three hats on the carpet with a shilling under each. "Hey, presto, cockolorum!" he cried. And lo! when he lifted the hats, all three of the shillings were found in a heap under one! George Coleman's heart was won!

It was way back in the lonely hamlet of Pallas, in Ireland, that Oliver Goldsmith was born, in a little old house that the peasant folk said stood on haunted ground, where "the good folk," the fairies, held their nightly revels. But when little Noll was still very young, his father moved to a better home on the outskirts of Lissoy. This home was part parsonage and part farm; for Father Goldsmith was a country curate, large of heart and small of means, and as guileless and ignorant of the world as the dear old Vicar of Wakefield. Lissoy was a charming village, with sheltered little white cottages and cultivated farms.

At the age of six little Noll was sent to the village schoolmaster, Thomas Byrne, and what a man he was! He had served in the Spanish wars, and now, when he should have been teaching the village urchins their sums, he held them spellbound with tales of his vagabond wanderings abroad, adventures of which he, himself, was usually the hero. To this he added tales of fairies, ghosts and banshees, pirates, robbers, smugglers. Indeed, little Noll imbibed in his youth far more of romance than of learning. When he grew older he was sent to a higher school at Edgeworthstown, some twenty miles from Lissoy, and on his last journey home from there, a mere stripling of sixteen, he met with a most absurd adventure.

Little used to money was Oliver Goldsmith, and now a friend had given him a whole round golden guinea to cover his traveling expenses. Noll's head was quite turned by his riches! Off he started on horseback over a road so rough as to be impassable to coaches, determined to play the man and spend his treasure in lavish fashion. For the night he halted at Ardagh, and, intending

to ask the whereabouts of the inn, he accosted the very first person he met, demanding with swaggering importance to know where was "the best house in the village." Now it chanced that the man whom he thus encountered was a famous wag and, amused by the stripling's importance, he directed him literally to "the best house in the village," the family mansion of one Mr. Featherstone, a gentleman of great fortune. With all the airs in the world, up rides young Noll to the house, which he thinks is an inn, and orders his horse to be led away to the stable! He then walks into the parlor, seats himself by the fire and curtly demands to know what he can have for supper! The owner of the place, seeing the lad's whimsical mistake, and learning by chance, that he was the son of an old friend, determined to carry out the joke. So young Goldsmith was fooled to the top of his bent and permitted to have full sway all the evening. Usually Noll was shy and diffident of manner, but thinking himself now among inferiors, he grew very free and easy, showing off and making out that he was a most experienced traveller. When supper was served he condescendingly insisted that the landlord, his wife and daughter should sit at the table and partake of the meal with him, and when he went to bed, as a last flourish of manliness, he gave special orders that a hot cake should be ready for his breakfast. Imagine his dismay next day when he learned he had swaggered thus in the house of a private gentleman! Years later he turned this ludicrous blunder into the play *"She Stoops to Conquer or The Mistakes of a Night,"* which set all London laughing.

But Goldsmith's school life, henceforth, was far from happy. He was ugly, awkward and poor, and, moreover, little given to learning. In Trinity College, Dublin, he had to earn his way by holding the position of a servant, and tutors and boys seemed in league together to jeer at and torment him.

Time and again he failed, failed, failed. He was to have entered the ministry, but he appeared before the Bishop to seek his appointment in such loud scarlet breeches that the Bishop was scandalized and sent him packing. He failed at the law; he failed as a student of medicine. So at last he took his flute and off he went alone for a walking tour through Flanders, France and Switzerland. As he journeyed he played on his flute and wherever he went his tunes earned for him his supper and a bed.

After wandering through Italy, likewise, Nolly returned to England with no friends and no calling. At length he took a garret in a dark, miserable, little back court that could only be reached by a steep flight of narrow flagstone stairs, called Breakneck Steps. Here washings hung out all day and frowsy women quarreled over the washtubs, but for the first time in his life Goldsmith set earnestly to work. He began to write, to drudge at writing, doing whatever the booksellers ordered. Now these were the days when hustling little John Newbery kept his far-famed shop in St. Paul's Churchyard, where the first real children's books were displayed, bound wood-cuts. Goldsmith did a great deal of work for Newbery, probably editing the first *Mother Goose* and writing the famous tale, *Goody Two-Shoes*.

Newbery's popular books, reprinted in America, 1749-1831, were widely read by children during the Revolution. In his honor, the Newbery medal is annually awarded to the best children's book by an American author.

But even in such dark days Goldsmith was never bitter. He was always inviting his landlady or some poor child into his rooms to cheer them with a cake or a sweetmeat and to play for them on his flute. Moreover, all his life long he believed with childlike simplicity anything that was told him, and many a tale of woe, either true or untrue, wrung from him his last penny. Sometimes, too, with that curious unworldliness that kept him from ever truly understanding money, he gave away things he did not possess. Once his landlady came to him with a sorry tale of her husband cast into the debtor's prison for desperate need of money. Moved to the heart, Goldsmith sold a new suit of clothes which he had not paid for, in order to give her the money. He was then called a knave and a sharper by those who had sold him the suit, and nearly went to the debtor's prison himself trying to pay for what he no longer possessed.

Slowly, slowly, however, his writings began to be noticed. Ah, now he commenced to make worthy friends! At length the great Dr. Samuel Johnson himself, the most famous literary light of the day, became his friend. In 1764 he was one of a group of most remarkable men who formed a club that met regularly, to talk over their coffee cups, at the Turk's Head Tavern. There was the big, burly Doctor Johnson, so important and high-and-mighty, and there, always tagging after him was his humble little toadie, James Boswell, forever delighting in being snubbed by the great Dr. Johnson. There was Edmund Burke, the brilliant Irish orator, to be known in the days of the American Revolution for his eloquent speech in Parliament on *Conciliation With the Colonies*, and there was the famous portrait painter, Sir Joshua Reynolds. The actor David Garrick, was likewise a friend of the group. All these great men loved their "Nolly," though they often made merciless fun of him.

One day word came to Dr. Johnson that Goldsmith was in great distress and besought him to come to his lodgings at once.

Off went Dr. Johnson to find that Goldsmith's landlady had had him arrested for failure to pay his rent and a sheriff's officer had him in custody. Goldsmith told Johnson, however, that he had the manuscript of a novel ready for print, but could not go out to sell it because of the officer. Johnson glanced hastily over the manuscript, saw that it had merit, and went out and sold it for sixty pounds ($300). That manuscript was the famous story, *The Vicar of Wakefield*.

Soon after this, Goldsmith's poem, *The Traveller*, appeared, and it was at once pronounced so fine that his friends at the Turk's Head could scarcely believe he had written it. Now, at last, Goldsmith began to prosper and to earn a great deal of money. But alas! funny little man that he was, he would still continue to make such ridiculous blunders. The Duke of Northumberland sent for him to congratulate him on *The Traveller*. Dressed in his best, Goldsmith sallied forth to Northumberland House, preparing on the way a lot of studied compliments to recite to his noble patron. After he had waited some time in Northumberland House a very grand personage appeared, most elegantly dressed. Taking him for the Duke, "Goldy" delivered unto him all the fine compliments he had prepared. To his great astonishment the gorgeously dressed individual informed him that he was only a servant, and his master would presently appear! As the Duke came in just then, he found Goldsmith so confused that, far from repeating his compliments, he could scarcely stutter a word.

During his latter days Goldsmith became famous and had such delightful friends as the Hornecks, a widow and two lovely daughters, one of whom, Miss Mary, he called affectionately, the Jessamy Bride. But in spite of his fame, he never learned how to manage money, and throughout his life he remained the same simple, kind-hearted gentleman whose friends, though they smiled at his blunders, always loved him so dearly.

In Goldsmith's time, the first novels were being written by Samuel Richardson, Henry Fielding, Lawrence Sterne, and Tobias Smollett. Goldsmith's *Vicar of Wakefield* was one of the earliest novels.

A Boy of the Lake Country*

WILLIAM WORDSWORTH (*English*, 1770-1850)

WHEN the river Derwent has left the mountains to mirror on its bright blue waters the ruins of old castle towers, it flows along the margin of a grassy terrace where once a little cottage stood.

In that cottage lived a boy of five whose playmate was the river. Through all the shining summer William Wordsworth bathed in the mill-race which was part of that beautiful stream. And the river, as it went meandering between green banks beneath the alder's shade, sang songs to him. When he was still a babe in arms, the music of its waters, murmuring over fords and shallows, gurgling over rocky falls, was blended with his nurse's song, and flowed through all his childish dreams.

Sometimes he scoured the sandy fields about the river, leaping through flowery groves of yellow ragwort, or, when rock and hill and wood, and the lofty height of distant Mt. Skiddaw were bronzed with deepest radiance, he stood alone beneath the sky like some small Indian savage, sporting naked on the plains.

*Told chiefly in Wordsworth's own words from his poem, *The Prelude*. Living in Wordsworth's time were the poets, William Cowper, author of *John Gilpin's Ride;* Thomas Hood, author of *Precocious Piggy;* and the mystic dreamer, William Blake, the first real poet of childhood.

Thus, in beloved spots about his home, the little fellow rambled till eight birthdays had gone by. And then his mother died; he bade his father and his sister Dorothy a long good-bye and left the town of Cockermouth where he was born, for school at Hawkshead in the lovely Esthwaite Vale. It was a kind and motherly old dame who kept the school there, and the boys, a noisy crew, were rich in happiness and joy.

When cold and frost were on the mountains, William, with a store of snares across his shoulder, ranged the open heights where woodchucks ran along the smooth green turf. Through half the night the boy would scud from snare to snare, alone beneath the moon and stars. And once in these night wanderings when he found his own snares empty, lo, he saw a bird held captive in a comrade's snare. Then, suddenly, the wish to have it overpowered him and he took it for his own. But when the shameful deed was done, he heard among the solitary hills low breathings coming after him and sounds of undistinguishable motion, steps almost as silent as the turf. And so it was that Nature spoke to him and woke his boyish heart to know the dark and haunting gloom that mars life's joy when one has done an act of wrong.

Again, upon a summer evening, he beheld a little boat tied to a willow tree and sheltered in a rocky cave. Straightway, he unloosed the chain, and, stepping in, pushed off from shore. It was an act of stealth and troubled pleasure, and the voice of mountain echoes, weird reproaches, followed him. But, aiming now to reach a chosen point with straight, unswerving line, he fixed his view upon the summit of a craggy ridge that seemed the far horizon's utmost edge. Above him were the gray sky and the stars, and, as he dipped his oars into the silent lake, his boat, an elfin pinnace, glided heaving through the water like a swan, and left behind on either side small circles glittering idly in the moon until they melted all into one track of sparkling light.

But on a sudden, from behind that craggy steep which had till then appeared to bound the sky, there loomed a peak, a huge, black peak. As if of its own power, it raised its huge black head. He rowed straight on, but that grim shape, growing still in stature, with purpose of its own, it seemed, and measured motion like a living thing, strode after him. With trembling oars, he turned, and through the silent water stole his way back to the covert of the willow tree. There, in her mooring place, he left his stolen boat, and went his way in grave and serious mood across the meadows homeward. And after that, for many days, there hung a darkness in his thoughts. No pleasant images of trees, of sea or sky remained, no colors of green fields, but only huge and mighty forms like that grim peak.

And by such discipline as this, the Spirit that is soul of all the universe spoke out through mountain, vale, and stream, and purified within the boy the elements of feeling and of thought.

It was a happy time for all the boys, when in the frosty Wintertime, the sun was set, and through the gloom for many a mile the cottage windows blazed. All shod with steel, they hissed along the polished ice in games, flying through the darkness and the cold. Then not a voice was idle, and the cliffs rang out, smitten with the din, the leafless trees and every icy crag tinkled like iron, while the stars to eastward sparkled clear, and in the west the orange sky of evening died away. But William, often leaving all the tumult of the throng, glanced sideways, quite alone into some little bay, to cut across the mirrored image of a star that fled and, flying still before him, gleamed upon the glassy plain.

The schoolboys lived in lowly cottages with only plain and homely comforts, yet they all pursued with eagerness their home amusements by the warm peat-fire. How many evenings did they sit around the snow-white table, head to head, absorbed in games of loo or whist, while out of doors incessant rain was falling, or the frost raged bitterly and far away, from under Esthwaite's splitting fields of ice, the pent-up air, struggling to free itself, gave out to meadows, groves, and hills, a loud protracted yelling, like the voice of wolves, howling in troops along the Bothnic Main.

From week to week, from month to month, they lived a round of tumult and ran a boisterous course. In summer they prolonged their games till daylight failed, no chair remained before the doorways, benches and threshold steps were empty, and even that old man who sat the latest lingerer, had gone indoors to bed. A mass of stone, standing midway in the square of the little market-village, was the center of these sports. Just here an old dame sat and watched her table with its hucksters' wares, where boys bought sweetmeats and small trinkets while the pennies in their pockets did not fail.

But, as time went on, every scheme of holiday delight, every boyish frolic, must be coupled with some winning form of Nature. Close to Hawkshead stretched Lake Windermere's long length, a universe of Nature's fairest forms,—lake, islands, promontories, gleaming bays! When summer came, the lads would race along Lake Windermere with rival oars. Their goal was now an island, musical with birds, now a sister isle where lilies of the valley grew beneath the shade of oaks, or now a third small isle, where still survived the ruins of an ancient church. In such a race what cared the boys who won? What room was there for jealousy or envy when the end was so delightful? All pleased alike, the conquered and the conqueror, they rested in the shade. Thus pride of strength and all vain glory of superior skill were tempered for young William, and there grew in him a quiet independence of the heart.

Now those were days when none among the boys was over-blest with pocket money. William's father, a solicitor of little means, had died when William was but thirteen years of age, and it was uncles who still kept the lad in school. But when the boys came back from holidays with weightier purses, they made merry with some rustic dinner on the cool green ground, or in the woods, or by a river side, and all the while among the leaves, soft airs were stirring, and the midday sun shone brightly round about them in their joy.

At other times, the lads drew largely from their funds and hired them horses from the innkeeper. Then they rode away to see the ruin of some famous temple where, long ago, the Druids worshipped in their circle of weird stones, or they sought an ancient abbey with its mouldering walls, its broken arch and belfry; and while their horses grazed along the smooth green turf, they rambled in the ruins, lingering a little by the knight in armor and the abbot carved in stone on ancient tombs, or hearkening perhaps while one small wren made melody through all those roofless, ivy-covered walls.

Their steeds remounted and the summons given with whip and spur, the boys would fly beyond the chapel walls and down the valley. Riding home the longest way through sheer delight in active limbs, they scampered on through rough and smooth, and now, along the margin of the moonlit sea, they beat with thundering hoofs the level sand.

Midway on long Winander's eastern shore, within the crescent of a pleasant bay, a tavern stood. Thither, in their little boat, the boys could row. It was no homely-featured house, primeval like its neighbor cottages. Indeed, it was a splendid place, the door beset with chaises, grooms and liveries, its sign-board glittering with characters in gold. The garden lay upon a slope surmounted by a bowling green. Beneath it stood a grove with gleams of water through the trees. There, on that bowling green, for half an afternoon the boys would play, and, whether skill prevailed or someone made a happy blunder in the game, 'twas quite the same,—their bursts of glee made all the mountains ring. But ere the night had fallen they returned at leisure in their boat across the shadowy lake, and at such times they often set the

minstrel of their troop ashore on some small island, gently rowing off to leave him making music with his flute alone upon the rock. And then, on William's mind, the calm and dead-still water lay as with a weight of pleasure, and the sky, never before so beautiful, sank down into his heart and held him like a dream.

Whether, then, he drank in joy from evening waters, from silver wreaths of curling mist, or from the sun that laid his beauty on the morning hills, the boy received so much from Nature and her over-flowing soul that all his thoughts were steeped in feeling, all things had life to him; there was no smallest stick or stone but had a voice to sing, and he saw blessings spread about him like a sea.

But now there came a day when William, grown a youth, must leave his boyhood's games behind, and for the first time saw the towers and pinnacles of Cambridge University above a dusky grove. His college was St. John's, and in the first of three old Gothic Courts he had a little room. Right underneath, the college kitchen made a humming sound, all intermixed with scolding and shrill notes of sharp command. Nearby, he had for neighbor, Trinity's great organ and her clock, which never failed to ring the quarters day or night.

It was a strange migration for a villager, a stripling of the hills. How he delighted in the motley spectacle,—gowns grave or gaudy, doctors, students, streets, courts, cloisters, flocks of churches, gateways, towers! And furthermore, as if the change had waited on some fairy's wand, at once behold him rich in moneys, and attired in splendid garb with hose of silk and hair all powdered white like rimy trees when frost is keen. He boasted, too, a lordly dressing gown with other signs of manhood that supplied the lack of beard. And soon the weeks went roundly on with invitations, suppers, wine and fruit.

Of college labors, of the lecture room, all studded round as thick as chairs could stand, of exercises, hopes, examinations, fears, small jealousies and triumphs, good or bad, the lad took little note. Such glory was but little sought by him and little won. But often he would leave his comrades and his books to pace the level field, and read the face of earth and sky. Aye, there he had a world that was his own, for he had made it, and it lived to him alone and to the God who sees into the heart.

And when his first vacation days had come, he visited again the spots he loved so well at Hawkshead. With a dog as comrade, a rough but faithful terrier, he roamed the hills. And in those days he found a new note in his heart, a fresh-awakened interest in the life of men, in grandams and in grandads, in rosy prattlers and in growing girls. With different eye he saw the quiet woodman in the woods, the shepherd on the hills.

Yet still a swarm of boyish schemes, gauds, feasts, revelry and dance kept him from quiet thought. His mind was then a parti-colored show of grave and gay, solid and light, short-sighted and profane. It chanced one time that he had passed the night in dancing mid a throng of maids and youths, old men and matrons. There was gaiety and mirth with din of instruments, and shuffling feet, and glancing forms, and glittering tapers. Ere the guests retired, the eastern sky was kindling and the cock had crowed. Then home through humble copse and open field young William went.

Magnificent the morning rose in memorable pomp. In front the sea lay laughing at a distance. The solid mountains shone, bright as the clouds and drenched in light, and in the meadows and the lower grounds was all the sweetness of a common dawn,—dews, vapors and the melody of birds, and workmen going forth to till the fields. Then to the brim the young man's heart was full. He made no vows, but vows were made for him, that he should be a dedicated spirit; he should sing in words to touch the heart of all mankind the song of lake and hill and field, of laborer and common-folk, and all the dignity of toil.

At length the Cambridge days were done, but still young William could not settle down in London-town to be a barrister, a churchman or a soldier as his aunts and uncles wished. France lured him forth, for those were wild and stirring days in France. It was the year of 1792. The common-people, rising after centuries of unjust burden, with a will to break the yoke of tyranny, were in the throes of revolution. The prison-fortress of the Bastille had long since been leveled to the ground. That haggard, hungry rout of women, with the Paris riff-raff at their heels, had already stormed Versailles and brought King Louis back to town.

So William found himself arrived in Paris when the city was alive with marching men and sound of martial music. As he walked the streets he stared and listened with a stranger's ears to hawkers and haranguers, party-mad, hissing with ardent eyes, in knots or pairs or single. Aye, he scanned them all, watched every hint of anger, and vexation and despite.

A band of military officers then stationed in the city were the chief of his associates, men well-born, the chivalry of France. They stood prepared for instant flight in line with other youths then crowding all the roads of France. Their purpose was to join the band of emigrants in arms upon the borders of the Rhine, to league with foreign foes, come back once more to France, crush out the Revolution and restore the King. He freely lived with these defenders of the Crown who sought to bring him over to their cause, but ah, there glowed within his heart the vision of a free Republic, one where all men stood on equal ground with equal opportunities for good. And so, erelong, he found himself a patriot, his heart was given to the people and his love was theirs, all theirs.

Among that band of officers was one of quite another mould, a champion of the people, and for that reason spurned by all the rest. This man was Wordsworth's friend and in his company he left the city with his pack upon his back, to tramp among the old chateaux and down the banks of that romantic stream, the Loire.

When week had followed week, and they were once again returned to Paris, great events had come to pass. The King had been dethroned, the host of foreigners and emigrants had been defeated, a republic had now been proclaimed in France. And Wordsworth often passed the prison where the poor unhappy monarch with his wife and children lay, or saw the palace of the Tuileries, so lately stormed with roar of cannon by a furious host. There had been crimes, he knew it. There had been massacres in which the senseless sword was prayed to as a judge. How wrong was such a course, and yet in spite of what the people were through ignorance, young William's heart was all aflame to join their cause. The hate of tyranny laid hold on him and pity for the abject multitude. He wished to see men free, and willingly would he have given up his life to make them so. The youthful stir of fighting rebels thrilled his heart.

And then, one day, came word in haste from England. Aunts and uncles had no mind to let the youth involve himself in foreign wars. They stopped his small allowance, and sent word that not another penny should be his until he came back home.

What was he then to do, this youthful rebel? In a little time he found himself once more in London, sore, indeed, in heart. And now there came three years of deep depression and no peace. He could not find his place in life; he could not find his work, and over there in France, the cause of liberty which he so loved, brought shame upon itself with hideous crimes and terrors, till at last, Frenchmen, from oppressed, became oppressors, and in turn changed a war of self defence to one of conquest, losing sight of all that they had struggled for. So William almost lost his confidence in men.

And in that time of trouble, it was Dorothy, his sister, who preserved him still a poet, she who had tramped beside him many miles on long vacation days and found her way close to his heart.

"William, be a poet," she would say. "That only is your office here on earth."

So William turned his back on London, and they went away together to the countryside to seek the joy of calm and quiet thought. And there he labored to express himself in verse, but little that he wrote brought any praise from others. Only faithful Dorothy encouraged and sustained him. And then, one day came Samuel Coleridge a-knocking at his door! Ah, here at last was one to feel with him, a poet, too, to know his poet's soul. The warmest friendship now began between the two, and Dorothy and William left their little home to take a house hard by the cottage of their new-found friend.

Henceforth the two young men were much together, and each could tell the other all his inmost aims and dreams. A volume of their ballads soon appeared in print, wherein *The Ancient Mariner* by Coleridge, that weird, unearthly tale of sin and persecution, stood side by side with Wordsworth's simple, peasant poems, verses done in words so simple that the critics, used to high-flown subjects and the most elaborate of phrasing, could but lift their eyebrows in surprise and cry: "Is this stuff poetry?"

"Indeed!" asserted one. "This is an endless wilderness of twaddle!"

"Not a line of poetry," another said, "or scarce of common sense!"

And yet the two young friends were not disturbed by criticism of this sort. With steady aim, they still pursued their course. It was agreed that Wordsworth should continue seeking all his subjects from the commonplace, from daily life, should make men feel the joy in wood and stream and field, in simple tenderness and common duties. But Coleridge, in opposite wise, should cast across the common things of life, the weird and wizard twilight of his ghostly fancy.

Now in another year, William sought again with Dorothy the dearly loved Lake Country of his youth. They took a little cottage built of stone, just overlooking Grasmere's tiny gleaming eye, a crystal-shining lake, set like a gem within a circle of green hills. There in the utmost quiet and simplicity they lived. Sometimes they sat together in their little garden, watching birds and butterflies, and talking underneath a spreading tree. Again, they had their tea, quite cozy, in the sitting room, and toasted bread themselves before the open fire. It was a warm and tender love that bound these two. They understood each other perfectly. Of all their simple daily doings Dorothy kept record in her journal, busy little housewife that she was. At times, however, even such a busy housewife found an opportunity to write her thoughts, like William's, down in poetry.

All in good time, to make the poet's quiet happiness complete, a certain pretty maiden, Mary Hutchinson, she who had flitted in and out of Wordsworth's life, a phantom to adorn a moment, came to be his wife and live forevermore an inmate of his heart. And Coleridge and Robert Southey lived together just across the hills at Keswick. What, indeed, could friendship ask for more? Wordsworth, Southey, Coleridge, old friends, dear friends,—the Poets of the Lakes.

Thus fifty years went by while Wordsworth lived in Grasmere Vale, now in the little cottage at the northern end and later still at Rydal Mount, a pretty ivy-covered house with shady terraced lawn.

It was his little daughter Dora whom he held up in the garden of his home to see the "kitten on the wall sporting with the leaves that fall." As Dora grew, she played with Edith Southey and with Sara Coleridge. These three young things were constantly together. What a pretty triad, linking closer still the hearts of their three fathers!

Aye, Wordsworth lived to see his children's children play

about his knees at Rydal Mount. And then, one day, there came a message in his letter bag. The Queen, Victoria herself, had summoned him to London. He should be her Poet Laureate! What greater honor could be showered upon a poet? Off he went to London, dear old man, all in a suit of borrowed clothes that were a size or two too small and scarcely let him straighten up his back when he had made his bow before the Queen. For, ah, his income had been always meager, and he had no guineas left to spare for courtier's clothes. However that might be, it mattered not. The world had come at last to know his real worth and honor it. He was no wild, rebellious, forceful soul like Byron or like Shelley, for the man had grown in years beyond the youthful days of wild rebellion, but he was a calm and quiet soul, the very spirit of serenity, who saw the glory of God's world, who felt it deep within his heart, who never, though he traveled far in years, lost sight of that immortal sunlit sea where children sport forever on the shore.

I Wandered Lonely as a Cloud
Lines Written in March
To the Cuckoo
The Sparrow's Nest
We are Seven
To a Butterfly

HALLS OF FAME

A Wizard of the Twilight

SAMUEL TAYLOR COLERIDGE (*English*, 1772-1834)

HALF way up a wooded hill near a little village in Devon is a cave called the Pixies' Parlor. Its ceiling is formed by the roots of ancient trees, all black with age and weirdly intertwined. Within those dusky depths, good housewives tell their bairns, the pixies dwell; and from that place, when the moon fades shadowy pale, and clouds go scudding across the sky, they issue forth to dance.

A boy once loved the witchery of that fantastic spot. Samuel Taylor Coleridge,—he carved his name upon its walls and there he dreamed of pixies, and all the pranks they play beneath the midnight moon.

Samuel was the son of a poor clergyman of Ottery Saint Mary, and he was the youngest of ten children who crowded the little old vicarage almost to bursting. It was a pretty village where he was born, with an old church tower whose bells made music all day long. Over the fresh green fields around the town he loved to ramble, down flowery lanes, or along by the river Otter, where tall tree-shadows slept on the quiet waters. But, as he rambled, he was not Samuel Coleridge, the clergyman's son, at all. He was St. George delivering the world from the dragon. In vivid fancy he went through all the moving details of that heroic story, and when it came to cutting off the head of the dragon, he felt himself to be St. George with such terrific vim that he took his stick and slashed off the heads of all the weeds that grew by the roadside.

But when Samuel was only ten years old his father died, and, as his family was poor, his little belongings were all bundled up, and he was packed off to a charity school, called Christ's Hos-

pital, in London. And now he roamed no more the flowery fields and lanes of Devon. Clad in a long blue coat with yellow stockings, the uniform of the school, he found himself a dweller in the city, pent up among gray walls, where he saw nothing lovely except the sky and stars.

He was, indeed, a miserable little fellow, pale and half-starved, neglected and sometimes whipped. His only escape from such wretchedness was in the magic of his fancy, and, as he walked the streets of London, he dreamed just as he had in Devon.

One day he was walking along the crowded Strand, fancying that he was Leander swimming the Hellespont. Quite blind to the throng of people pressing about him he began taking strokes with his arms to accomplish his feat in swimming. Suddenly a man's voice cried: "Stop, you young thief!"

There stood an angry old gentleman to waken the lad from his dream. In a flourish of his swimming Samuel had touched his coat, and the stranger was convinced that the shabby little rascal had meant to pick his pocket.

"Ah, sir," cried Samuel, "I did not mean to touch your pocket. I thought I was Leander swimming the Hellespont!"

Well! Well! Well! The old gentleman opened his eyes and steadied his glasses and looked curiously at the boy before him. But soon he was bending over to question the lad with interest, and when he discovered how poor he was, and that he longed more than anything else in the world for books, he was touched to the depths of his kindly heart, and bought the boy a subscription to a circulating library. Thereafter, Samuel, being no less hungry in mind than he was in stomach, devoured these books with eagerness, and they nourished his dreams and visions.

For eight long years Samuel lived at the charity school in London, but when he was eighteen means were found to send him to Cambridge University. Under the shadow of those classic old gray towers, he proved a brilliant student in all literary subjects.

On a certain winter evening he was supping with a college friend, when, on leaving for home, he carelessly took away with him a book called "The Robbers," by the German poet, Schiller. A winter midnight, the wind high, and "The Robbers" to read for the very first time! Though there was not a single goblin in all the tale, it gave Samuel the most delicious creeps, and filled him with splendid horrors. And then, with all a boy's love for such uncanny thrills, he longed to be the wizard who could conjure up moods like that, and move men out of the humdrum to feel as he felt that night.

But if Samuel loved all literary subjects, alack for mathematics! He loved mathematics not at all. Mathematics were to him a bugbear. And so, as time passed, what with this and other troubles, he grew more and more discontented, and one fine day he left college and ran away to join the army.

Now behold Master Samuel Coleridge, having taken the name of Comerback which he chanced at the moment of enlistment to see over the door of a shop, a private in the dragoons! And an awkward private he was! He could not ride a horse; he could not even rub down his horse; he could not learn to drill. In fact, he was Chief of the awkward squad, and in such a situation he was very unhappy, indeed. He spent much time in the public tap-room of the inn at Reading, wrapped deep in thought, and there, 'mid the flaring lights and the boisterous noise of the common soldiers who were drinking at tables about him, he composed a poem called *Religious Musings*, a very strange poem certainly to have issued from a tap-room.

At length, one day, when his unhappiness seemed more than he could bear, he wrote on the white wall of the stables, just beneath his saddle, the following sentence in Latin:

"Alack! how miserable it is for those who are unfortunate to have been happy!"

Soon the captain of the troop came along and saw the sentence. "Well, well!" said he to himself. "What man among the private soldiers is scholar enough to write a sentence in Latin?" And he enquired of a dragoon standing by whether he knew to whom the saddle belonged.

"Please, your honor, to Comerback," answered the dragoon.

"Comerback," said the Captain, "send him to me."

In a short time Comerback presented himself and saluted with the inside of his hand in front of his cap.

His officer said mildly: "Comerback, did you write the Latin sentence which I have just read under your saddle?"

"Please, your honor," answered the soldier, "I wrote it."

"Then, my lad," said the Captain, "you are not what you appear to be," and thinking that a youth of so much education did not belong among the common soldiery, he added: "I shall speak to the commanding officer, and you may depend on my speaking as a friend."

Accordingly, Comerback was taken before the General and

when it was discovered that he had been a student at Cambridge and had run away to enlist, he was given his discharge. Soon a chaise appeared at the door of the Bear Inn, Reading; the officers of the Fifteenth cordially shook the young man's hand, and off he drove, not without a tear, along the Bath road to London and Cambridge.

But, though Coleridge returned to Cambridge, he soon left the university a second time without obtaining a degree. And now he formed an enthusiastic friendship with two other young poets, Robert Southey and Lovell, the Quaker.

Southey was an eager young fellow who had passed his boyhood at the home of an aunt, reading and writing plays. When he was in school at Westminster, he had proved his independence by writing an essay against flogging, for which he had been promptly expelled from the institution. Coleridge met Southey just after he had left Oxford University where he had studied for two years.

Now those were the days when the common people, across the channel in France, had risen against the tyranny of their kings, had declared themselves for liberty, equality and brotherhood, and established a republic in place of their age-old kingdom. These events stirred the three young men in England to the very depths of their souls.

"A republic of brotherhood and equality is the ideal state for all men," they declared, and they put their heads together and worked out a wonderful plan. They would cross the ocean to America; on the banks of the Susquehanna River they would found an ideal state. There all men should be equal, all men should be brothers, selfishness should be no more, and goodness should reign supreme. Each one, for a short work day, should follow the plough or do the necessary labor, but when evening came, they would gather around the poets of the crowd, and hang enraptured on their songs.

It was a dream that fired all three with eagerness. Nothing was lacking save the small matter of funds to carry out the scheme. With earnest enthusiasm they set to work at once lecturing and writing to raise sufficient money.

And then an event occurred. The two young enthusiasts, Coleridge and Southey, suddenly fell in love with the sisters of Lovell's wife, the enchanting Misses Fricker! And there was a pretty kettle of fish! Instead of setting sail for America, they found themselves with wives on their hands! Instead of working out the problems of an Ideal State, Coleridge had to face the problem of earning a living, of raising corn and vegetables enough from a little farm to support himself and his wife, as well as a couple of pigs. Thus ended the dream of the Ideal State.

But now in the course of a summer excursion, Coleridge made a new friend, who throughout his life was dearer than any other. He called on the young poet, Wordsworth, who was living with his sister, Dorothy, in a small country house in Dorsetshire. Each was charmed with the other, and so strong was their mutual liking that Wordsworth and Dorothy soon moved to Alfoxden, to be near Coleridge at Nether Stowey.

Henceforth the friends spent many happy days in delightful intercourse, now sitting on the grass by the brink of a stream in the most beautiful part of the most beautiful glen of Alfoxden, now in Wordsworth's little garden, or over his cheery tea-table, where the faithful Dorothy was a comrade and inspiration to both. It was a joy to each to confide to the other his thoughts and the poems he was planning.

One afternoon, Coleridge, Wordsworth and Dorothy started out on a walking tour to visit Lenton and the Valley of Stones. As they had very little money among them, Coleridge and Wordsworth agreed to defray the expenses of the tour by writing a poem, which they hoped they might sell to the New Monthly Magazine for the price of five pounds. They were tramping along

the Quantock Hills towards evening, when Coleridge said that a friend of his had had a dream which he would like to embody in this poem. It was to be a spectral sort of tale, the story of an old navigator, who had committed some crime which should bring upon him a ghostly persecution and the punishment of endless wandering, but Coleridge did not know what crime to make the old man commit. Now it chanced that a day or two before this, Wordsworth had been reading a book of Voyages in which it related how mariners, doubling Cape Horn, frequently saw albatrosses, the largest sort of sea-fowl, some extending their wings twelve or fifteen feet.

"Suppose," suggested Wordsworth, "that you represent this old mariner as having killed one of those birds on entering the South Sea, and that the tutelary spirits of those regions take upon them to avenge the crime."

Coleridge thought the incident fit for his purpose and so began the "Rime of the Ancient Mariner," the blood-curdling tale of the man who shot the harmless albatross that loved and trusted him, and so brought upon himself the ghastly punishment decreed by the Lonesome Spirit from the South Pole, who "loved the bird that loved the man, who shot him with his bow."

As the two young men proceeded trying to compose the poem together, Wordsworth soon discovered that this goblin rout of horror was a subject unfit for his own peculiar gift, which dwelt steadily in the sunshine, so he withdrew from the undertaking and left Coleridge to carry it out alone.

After a few days the friends returned from their delightful

tour, but already the Ancient Mariner had grown beyond all the bounds of their expectations when they thought to compose a poem which might fetch them five pounds. Instead, they now began to talk of a volume of poems, chiefly on subjects taken from common life, but looked at through the transforming mist of imagination and fancy. This volume soon appeared under the name of *Lyrical Ballads.*

And now the difference in the work of the two young men became ever more apparent. Wordsworth loved the commonplace, Coleridge the supernatural, and, if Wordsworth's poems seemed to be always in the sunlight, those of Coleridge were in a wizard twilight. Coleridge loved the night, he loved all the breathless stillness of a frosty midnight with "silent icicles quietly shining to the moon." Often he carried little Hartley, his baby boy, out in his arms to show him the evening star, and bid him hark to the song of the nightingale, that with the night he might associate joy, and once when the child awoke crying from a dream, he hurried with him to the orchard, and showed him the moon. Then the baby, hushed at once, suspended his sobs and laughed most silently while his eyes, swimming with undropped tears, glittered in the moonbeam.

But, alas! There soon came a time when Coleridge left his little son, his wife and family, and passed through the depths of a miserable experience. He had begun to take opium to relieve him of pain, and the habit of taking the drug grew steadily upon him until he became its victim, and could not resist it. Then the kindly Robert Southey took Coleridge's wife and children into his home at Keswick amid the hills of England's beautiful Lake Country. Southey had already assumed the care of his old friend Lovell's widow and child, so, with his own children, it was a large and expensive household of which he was pater familias.

And now, in his battles with the demon, opium, Coleridge often wandered away from his home, and all his loved ones, sad and miserable, and most a stranger at his own hearth-fire.

It was Uncle Southey who took up Samuel's duties. It was he who labored incessantly to support all those dependent upon him. In his great library, bulging with books, he was always at work, writing, writing, writing, a daily walk with his family his only recreation, and the children playing about, tripped over Greek and Latin tomes, or kept house in caves made of venerable old Spanish and Icelandic chronicles.

Wordsworth now lived near by at Grasmere, and the children of these three families were constantly together. Sometimes the Southey family and the Wordsworth family met half way between the two homes and picnicked in some beautiful spot. Often, too, they visited the Falls of Lodore, where Southey's little boy asked him how the water came down.

For fifteen long years Coleridge struggled with the opium habit, and he never came back again to settle down and live with his wife and children. In 1816 he entered the home of a Mr. Gillman at Highgate where he lived all the rest of his life, another eighteen years. Here he finally succeeded in conquering his devil, but he did not again become a man of keen and eager vitality. It was during his years in the Lake Country that he produced the best of his work, and Coleridge, Wordsworth and Southey, are called the Lake School of poets. Nevertheless, few men have been more beloved, or admired, than Samuel Coleridge, for he thought deeply and spoke with brilliance, and to Highgate, as to some shrine, came all the younger men of letters.

Coleridge is best known for those poems in which he produced "the creeps" which he himself had so much enjoyed on the night he read *The Robbers*. In all English literature there are no more "creepy" poems than *Christabel* and the *Rime of the Ancient Mariner*. He was indeed a wizard who conjured up goblins with his weird, unearthly melody.

The Rector's Son

ALFRED TENNYSON (*English,* 1809-1892)

SOMERSBY lay a mere dip of green in the treeless waste of hills. To the north stretched the wind-swept wolds, to the south the wide sadness of the fens, to the east the marshes moaning in the gale. In contrast to all this bleakness the gentler beauties of nature that showed themselves at Somersby touched with a deeper feeling the heart of Alfred Tennyson, the Rector's little son—violets and cuckoo flowers, warmth and scent and color, the song of birds and the music of running water.

Above the lane, deep sunken in flowery banks, rose the squat little church, small and unpretentious beneath its yew trees, the slim Gothic cross among the gravestones its only claim to beauty. Directly opposite stood the Rectory, a tiny house built of white-washed brick covered with woodbines, and nestling beneath a mass of elms and larches that dappled the lawn with sun and shade. How in the world could seven lanky boys, four girls, a father, a mother, an occasional aunt, indefinite servants and intermittent guests all squeeze themselves into a building so small?

Alfred was a lean dark little fellow with a firm-set, leonine head and a mane of thick hair. When he was very little he would put words together into lines which pleased him and run about shouting, "Far, far, away!" or "I heard a whisper in the wind." At eight he covered two sides of a slate with blank verse. At twelve he had composed an epic in twelve books which he would go shouting about the fields in the dark.

Alfred was not happy in school. He preferred the hollyhocks and lilies and friendly faces of the Rectory, and so he was taught largely at home by his father. Up in the attic he had a favorite room, clean and white, with dimity curtains and the smell of honeysuckle, and the hooting of owls at night time. Here he and his brothers read to each other the poems they had written.

The Rector, a tall, stern man, was not pleased with his sons for writing poetry. Was that any way for a poor boy to earn a living, pray tell? But their mother, on the contrary, was thrilled by their ability. When she was dragged up the hills in her basket chair by a great Newfoundland dog—for she was often an invalid—she hearkened proudly while they read her the poems they had written, a pleasant little confederacy of mother and sons. One wonderful afternoon when Alfred was seventeen, Mrs. Tennyson stood at the cross-roads waiting for the carrier, and when he came jogging along in his cart, he left her a parcel of proof, marked *Poems by Two Brothers*. What an event! Alfred and Charles were really in print, and with ten pounds for their efforts!

At Cambridge Alfred continued making a music of words but critics were harsh and mocking, not encouraging like his mother. His greatest comfort in those days was his friendship with young Arthur Hallam. All too soon, Hallam died and Alfred, brooding his loss, wrote his great poem *In Memoriam*. For years the young man struggled, but in time he found himself the best loved poet in England. In the cozy days of Queen Victoria when life flowed smoothly but not too deeply, his poems were everywhere read. He became a friend of the Queen, was made Poet Laureate of England and ended his days as Lord Tennyson.

THE CITY CHILD THE PRINCESS IDYLLS OF THE KING

Sweet Peas and Grecian Urns

JOHN KEATS (*English*, 1795-1821)

MR. THOMAS KEATS, lively and energetic of countenance, drove up to the fine, old, red brick building with blooming gardens which housed Mr. Clarke's school at Enfield. He was in his trim and shining gig with his two little sons, John and George, by his side. John was seven, George was six, but John was much the smaller of the two, a very tiny fellow, still wearing the dress of a child,—frilled collar, short jacket with huge pearl buttons, and a cap with a tassel. Both boys were round-eyed and awestruck. They were going away to school for the first time in their lives and their mother was far away, ten miles off in London!

Mr. Thomas Keats kept a livery stable at the sign of the Swan and Hoop in London. He had coaches and gigs and very fine horses to let. Once he had been only head hostler, but he had married Frances Jenkins, the daughter of the owner, and so become in time the proprietor of the place. A lively young couple they were, those two, with ambition and imagination, stepping boldly on in the world. From living in rooms above the stable, they moved to a real house, where they entertained the rosiest dreams for the future of their sons. Thomas even had visions of sending the boys to Harrow, Harrow the aristocratic, the school for gentlemen's sons. But that was flying a bit too high. His purse was too small for that. He must needs clip the wings of ambition and be content with Enfield.

Accordingly, Mr. Keats deposited John and George and drove away. There they were, poor little shavers, dumped down alone to face seventy or eighty youngsters all ready to gape and jeer at them in the ugly fashion of the time. Here was little John Keats, a tiny slip of a child,—he would make good sport for the older boys perhaps! Not on your life! Little John could fight like a terrier. Morning, noon and night he was more than willing to fight. Let him only catch sight of a big boy tormenting another, and he would plunge into battle on the spot, never heeding though he stood like a Lilliputian against some blustering giant.

Once a tall usher boxed the ears of his youngest brother, Tom, who had then just entered school. Seeing what had happened, John rushed up like a little bantam cock, and putting himself in the proper attitude of defense, punched the astonished usher, who could easily have picked him up and put him in his pocket.

Such outbursts of fire, however, were but flame in a wisp of straw. They burnt out on the instant, for John was at heart an affectionate lad, never mean, and easily moved to any generous feeling.

The three boys, John, George and Tom, were still only little tads when their father was killed by a fall from his horse. And now their mother, whom they all dearly loved, was no longer able to keep the livery stable. She and her little daughter, Fanny, went to live with her mother in the country at Edmonton. Henceforth the boys saw no more of London. Their days revolved between Clarke School and Grandmother's house, two miles away.

On half holidays and vacations John loved to roam about the fields. He loved to bring home to his Grandmother's wild pets from the brooks and bushes,—goldfinches, tomtits, minnows and mice. Once he wrote of himself:

There was a naughty boy,
A naughty boy was he,
He kept little fishes
In washing tubs three,
In spite
Of the might
Of the maid,
Nor afraid,
Of his granny good!

Aye, in spite of the might of the maid who doubtless frowned darkly on the mess, they were indulgent women, that mother and grandmother. They let the boy keep his pets.

In those early days John cared not at all about winning high marks at school. A rough and tumble schoolboy was he, lively as the liveliest, passing his time with rambles, games and fights, and studying no more than was necessary just to scrape along. And then one day came his first great sorrow. The news had reached him. His mother was dead. Poor boy, he crept off and hid himself in desolation under the master's desk struggling pitifully with his grief. But after this he filled the void in his life with a sudden passion for books. He read all the time and he lived in his stories. Books, books, books,—he carried them with him everywhere, even to the table, and he fought all too valiantly if any one disturbed him.

Now at this time, "Granny good" was a very old lady and she had Fanny and the boys to think of. What would become of them after she was gone? She pondered this question often, and finally she decided to ask Mr. Richard Abbey, an old friend of hers, now a prosperous coffee merchant in London, to become their guardian. Poor Granny with all her good intentions! It was a sorry choice. Mr. Abbey had no more imagination than a cow, and he was so set in his ways that he would not exchange his knee-breeches for the long trousers which were the fashion of the day, until he became such an object of curiosity on the Exchange that everyone turned to look after him in his long white stockings and half boots. For John he had no use whatever. John was now fifteen, old enough to leave school,—so said Mr. Abbey. George and Tom he would take into his counting house in London, but John should be a surgeon, a good, honest, country doctor, riding around in a gig, pulling teeth, compounding pills and setting bones. John he apprenticed to Mr. Thomas Hammond, Surgeon, of Edmonton.

Henceforth John was a sort of handy house and stable boy,

making up medicines, tending shop, running errands, or going with his master to hold his horse on the rounds. In his leisure hours he walked back across the meadows to Enfield to read and chat in the arbor at the end of the garden with his old friend, Charles Cowden Clarke, the son of the Headmaster. Charles lent him books and copies of Leigh Hunt's paper, the *Examiner*. There was a man for boys to admire,—Leigh Hunt! Charles knew him personally, an independent, free-hearted fellow. One day this Hunt got himself sent off to jail for writing a violent article against the Prince Regent, afterwards George IV. Then Charles and John regarded him as a martyr and glowed with fiery indignation at this blow to the rights of free speech. Under the arbor the two youths also read Shakespeare together, and Charles let John take home a copy of Spenser's *Faery Queen*. Through the story of *Una and the Red Cross Knight* he ramped like a young horse through a spring meadow. It delighted him so completely that it called forth from him a poem, in *Imitation of Spenser*. From that day he loved writing more than anything else in the world.

John was only nineteen when his grandmother died, the last of the older generation who had loved and cherished him. His little sister, Fanny, went up to London to live with the Abbeys. His grandmother's house was closed and he, who so loved a home, was never to know another.

When the great day came that Leigh Hunt was let out of prison, Keats was overjoyed and keyed to a jubilee! He wrote a sonnet to Hunt and dashed off with it to find Clarke. Clarke was just setting out to walk up to London and congratulate the martyr. Keats met him and walked part way with him. At the gate to the last field when about to take leave of his friend, he grew embarrassed and self conscious, and with a look of hesitation, gave Clarke the sonnet. This was the first time Clarke had known that John was writing poetry.

After this, John began to chafe at his life as a surgeon's apprentice. He longed to kick over the traces and dash up to London. True, he still intended to be a surgeon and to give only leisure time to poetry, but he dreamt day in and day out of adventuring in literary by-ways of the city. Richard Abbey was disgusted and advised him to waste no more time in scribbling. Nevertheless, John persisted and one fine day saw him free of Hammond and walking up to London to pursue his studies in the hospitals, feeling like a knight setting forth on a thrilling adventure.

He was a handsome fellow in those days, John Keats, though still only five feet tall. The form of his head was like that of a fine Greek statue. His hair was red and his eyes a brilliant brown. In London he and his brothers made many pleasant friends, for all three young men bore themselves with true simplicity and distinction.

When he was off on a holiday nothing seemed to escape him, the song of a bird, the rustle of some little animal, the changing lights and the furtive play of shadows, the motions of the wind, the

wayfaring of the clouds, even the features and gestures of passing tramps. Certain things affected him extremely, particularly when he heard afar off, the wind coming across the woodlands. "The tide! The tide!" he would cry delightedly and spring on some stile or up on the low boughs of a wayside tree, and watch the passage of the wind on the meadow grasses, not stirring till the flow of air was all around him, while an expression of rapture made his eyes gleam. From fields of oats or barley rippling in the wind, it was almost impossible to drag him. Ah, the young fellow was in love with beauty. Already in his heart the refrain was ringing:

"Beauty is truth, truth beauty,—that is all
Ye know on earth and all ye need to know."

In those days he wrote a poem, *I Stood Tiptoe Upon a Little Hill.* It was all alight with his eager love of beauty. The clouds were in it and sweet buds in the morning dew, and the little noiseless noise that creeps among the leaves. How, pray tell, did he ever catch and hold the fragile, fairy-like beauty of sweet peas without weighing them down to earth by his words?

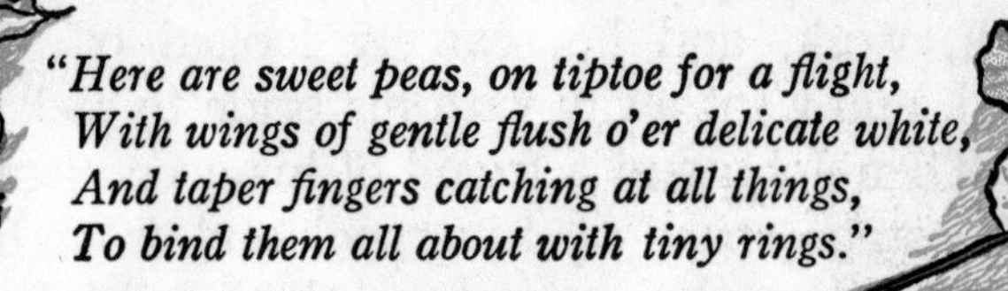

"Here are sweet peas, on tiptoe for a flight,
With wings of gentle flush o'er delicate white,
And taper fingers catching at all things,
To bind them all about with tiny rings."

There is all the airy delicacy of sweet peas forever set down in verse.

One day Clarke told Keats that Leigh Hunt intended to publish one of his sonnets in the *Examiner.* Three cheers! To be really in print at last! It was an enormous step forward! Moreover, Hunt invited Keats out to Hampstead to his home in the Vale of Health. His house was small and nearly as bursting with children as that of the *Old Woman Who Lived in a Shoe,* but he was warmly hospitable, and brilliant company was always gathered there, among them sometimes Shelley. True, Keats was not particularly drawn to Shelley. He thought the fiery youth with his bristling ideas for reforming the world somewhat of a crank, for Keats himself was the sanest, best balanced of men, never carried off headlong by a runaway of ideas. He had no wish to reform the world. He only wanted with all his heart to express his love of beauty. Nevertheless, Shelley appreciated Keats, and after his death, wrote a splendid poem in his honor.

In the Vale of Health there were fun and fancy, frolic and earnest, with endless readings and discussions. Keats was enchanted with it all, and was always running out to enjoy it. But now as his interest in poetry grew, he was more and more disturbed at thought of being a surgeon.

"The other day during the lecture," he said, "there came a sunbeam into the room and with it a whole troop of creatures floating in the ray, and I was off with them to Oberon and fairyland."

How could such a man be a surgeon? It was impossible! Much to Richard Abbey's disgust, Keats gave up at last and decided to devote himself only to poetry. He set himself seriously to work, —work, work, work, and he scarcely looked off until George Keats married, and went away with his bride to seek his fortunes in America. Then John and a friend of his accompanied the two on top of the stage coach to Liverpool and from there set off on a walking tour through Scotland and the English Lake Country where Wordsworth had his home. One day they tramped through that wild part of Scotland where the old gypsy, Meg Merrilies, had often boiled her kettle among fragments of rock and bramble and broom. Magic! Keats must write a ballad of Old Meg! When it was finished he sent it in a letter to his sister, Fanny, in London.

All in good time he arrived in Hampstead again, brown and shabby, with scarcely any shoes left, his jacket torn, a fur cap on his head, a Scotch plaid over his shoulder, and his knapsack on his back. Here he found that his brother Tom was desperately ill. Sad weeks followed, weeks of patient nursing, but in the end Tom died, and now, with George far away in America, he who so loved his brothers had no brothers left to comfort him. In those dark days, too, came the dreadful reviews of his first long poem, *Endymion.* The reviewers in *Blackwood's* and the *Quarterly Magazine* hated Leigh Hunt because he had criticized the Prince, and in order to strike at him, they smashed his friend with a withering irony and scorn. *Endymion* according to them was no more than the most ridiculous twaddle. Keats was cut to the heart. Moreover, he was in love with a handsome young woman, Fanny Brawne, and all his hope of marrying depended on his succeeding, that he might earn enough to support her.

He worked with a feverish energy. In times past an artist friend of his had taken him to the British Museum to see the splendid collection of old Greek sculptures, so dignified, graceful and simple in the clear-cut, white purity of marble. Keats was overcome at the sight. It meant to him a glorious revelation of beauty. Such beauty as that he wanted in his poems! Indeed, no man has ever written in English more beautiful lines than Keats. Had the critics only seen it! But no, they looked at his faults alone. They were blind and deaf to his genius.

One disappointment followed another. He strove and strove to succeed, but the reviewers knew no pity. Then one day he fell ill. After months of struggle he went off to Italy and died, alone save for one faithful friend.

Later generations have judged his work more truly. Graceful and beautiful as a Grecian urn, fragile and delicate as sweet peas, was the genius of little John Keats.

The Rebel

PERCY BYSSHE SHELLEY (*English*, 1792-1822)

THE rebel stood with his back against a wall, a slender lad, his blue eyes flashing fire, his hair wildly dishevelled. Round about him pressed a pack of Eton boys like hounds with a stag at bay.

"Shelley! Shelley! Mad Shelley!" shouted the tormentors. And they pinched him, they plucked at his jacket, and tore at his clothes. They nailed him to the wall with their muddy balls; one jerked the book from under his arm and kicked it into the mire.

"Shelley! Shelley! Mad Shelley!"

The grim old walls of Eton re-echoed with those cries.

Shelley's cheeks grew white, his whole body trembled and shook. He fought, he scratched, he slapped. It was all so unjust,—a dozen against one.

But the young hounds did not cease their sport until they had wearied of it and turned away to seek other game. Then Shelley picked up his mud-stained book and went back defiantly to his favorite haunt by the river.

Why was he "Mad Shelley"? Why? And why did the boys torment him? Because he was a rebel, a young rebel in a smug old world that was quite content with itself and had no wish to change a single one of its time-honored ways of thinking. Because he thought for himself, and his ideas ran contrary to the smooth flow of accepted standards and customs.

Eton College in those days was a school for the sons of country gentlemen and merchant princes. These worthy gentlemen expected that their sons would grow up, all thinking the same perfectly safe thoughts and patterned after the same perfectly proper mould, like so many china mandarins made to bob their heads one way only. None of your rebels here! The French Revolution had just proved how dangerous to the peace and comfort of the upper classes were republican ideas. In order to crush out any possibility of such thoughts, the young aristocrats of Eton were trained in a manner best calculated to turn out hard-faced men, well able to return a blow for a blow, but perfectly content with the ready-made ideas ground out for them and scarcely able to think dangerous or original thoughts for themselves. Indeed, if such a thought but showed signs of budding, there was Dr. Keate, the head-master of Eton, with his big stick, ready to flog the offender until he came to his senses.

"Boys, be pure in heart, for if you're not I'll flog you until you are!" That was Dr. Keate's way of insuring obedience to the Sixth Beatitude.

As to the boys themselves, they were all their fathers could wish. They neither questioned nor challenged the customs of Eton College. Indeed, they felt a pride in carrying on the traditions of a school that had been founded by Kings and was under the protection of royalty, even though these traditions were worthy only of savages.

Chief among the time-honored customs of Eton was one whereby all the little boys became slaves or "fags" to the big ones. The fag was obliged to make his master's bed, to pump the water for his bath and carry it up to him in the morning, to brush his clothes and clean his shoes. Disobedience was visited with terrible punishments. One boy, in order to force his fag to jump a ditch which was too wide for him, put spurs on his shoes. Every time the little fellow shrank back from the ordeal, he dug the spurs into him till the child's legs were bleeding and his new clothes torn to tatters.

On the very first day that Percy Shelley appeared in school, he decided that fagging was an outrage to human dignity and he refused to obey the orders of his fag-master. The Sixth Form Captains, seeing how slenderly and delicately he was built, thought that it would be easy enough to enforce their authority over him. But they soon discovered their mistake. They could threaten and bully and torment him, but they could not make him obey them.

Henceforth, Shelley did everything that was wrong according to the code of Eton. He loved books, he cared little about cricket and football, he hated bullying and that brutal spirit of which Eton was so proud. He went about with his long hair floating in the wind and his collar wide open, and he pronounced the strangest opinions on a variety of subjects. For all these reasons Shelley was proclaimed an outlaw. For all these reasons he was contemptuously dubbed Mad Shelley.

Today he lay on the grass by the quiet Thames and thought of the cruelty that had just been so wantonly showered upon him. Sunlight quivered over the meadows, clouds drifted peacefully in the far blue, the river made a low soft music as it glided past, and the willows, trailing their graceful branches in the breeze, bowed to their delicate reflections that floated tremulously in the stream. Before him, across the river, rose the walls and towers of Windsor Castle high above the trees. It was all so beautiful and still. Only from the somber cloisters of Eton College behind came the harsh noises of those who had been his tormentors. Pressing his hands together the young boy made this vow: "I swear to be just and wise and free if such power in me lies—I swear never to become an accomplice, even by my silence, of the selfish and the powerful. I swear to dedicate my whole life to the worship of beauty."

Now Percy was the son of a rich Sussex landowner, Mr. Timothy Shelley, and their home was Field Place in Sussex, a low, white house, standing in the midst of a well-kept park, beyond which stretched the dusky depths of an extensive woodland. The boy's grandfather, Sir Bysshe Shelley, an eccentric old fellow, had made Percy his heir to the exclusion of all the other children, but Percy was as little concerned about the possession of riches as the birds of the air. He wanted only to be free, free to think his own thoughts and express them.

Poor Mr. Timothy Shelley knew not what to make of such a son, always bubbling over with strange ideas and stirring up the monkeys. He himself held just those opinions on every subject which a country gentleman was expected to hold. In appearance he was tall and imposing and he doled out commonplace phrases with a ridiculous air of importance. Poor Mr. Timothy Shelley! Poor Mr. Timothy Shelley. No hen who has hatched a duckling was ever more at sea than he. He would have liked to bottle up his son, and he read him long and solemn lectures on the evil of his ways, but alack! he could not get the cork in tight enough to keep Percy's spirit from overflowing. As to Percy's mother, the beautiful Mrs. Shelley, she, like other ladies of her day, preferred a man to fight with his fists, rather than his mind, and it was with sad misgivings that she beheld him go for a ramble in the woods carrying with him a book instead of a gun.

While Shelley's elders were thus disturbed about him, however, he was in the eyes of his four little sisters and his cousin, Harriet Grove, nothing short of a hero. The moment he reached home from Eton he began to fill the house with the most fantastic, yet enthralling of guests,—hobgoblins and demons, witches and ghosts. He made the shadowy aisles of the park come to life with the haunting footsteps of elfin sprites flitting through the greenwood. He thrust his stick into every hole in the old walls, searching for secret passages that should lead to some strange world of ancient romance. In the attic of the house he discovered unexpectedly a locked room.

"Here," he whispered, "lives an old alchemist with a long beard, the terrible Cornelius Agrippa!"

And if there chanced to be heard a noise in that same mysterious attic, he would cry:

"It's Cornelius upsetting his lamp!"

Thus the little girls were kept in a continual state of delicious terror. And what made Percy's tales so enchanting was the fact that he almost believed them himself.

In addition to all this, Percy sought thrilling adventures in the wonderful Land of Science. Somewhere he had procured a machine which had just been invented and gave electric shocks. With this he went about "shocking" the girls, all of whom were delighted except the youngest, Helen, and she began to cry whenever she saw him appear with a bottle and bit of wire.

His most faithful followers were his eldest sister, Elizabeth, and his lovely cousin, Harriet Grove. These three were writing a novel together, and they called the book Zastrozzi. It was filled with the wild and hair-raising adventures of a haughty tyrant, a robber chief, and a beautiful lily-pure heroine. The favorite spot to which Shelley led these young girls when he wished to converse with them was the graveyard, which was surrounded for him with a mysterious fascination. There, between Harriet and Elizabeth, he seated himself on some ancient tomb in the shadow of the old gray church and talked to his heart's content about everything under the sun.

It was as easy as A, B, C, from Percy's standpoint, to separate

the good from the bad in life. There on one side of the fence were all the bad people, those who had power over others and exercised it tyranically, and there on the other side, as plain as the nose on your face, were the good, that is, the philosophers, the poor and the weak. He saw no use for laws to make men good. Goodness and love and purity should be in men's hearts. They should be free as the air, free to be true to the beauty in their own souls. Laws all seemed to him to be more or less like the big stick with which the Headmaster of Eton sought to flog the boys into purity. No man should have power to compel another. It was an indignity to be compelled. Young as he was, it never entered his boyish head that, since men were by no means pure in heart as yet, they would get into a fine mess if there were, for the present, no outward laws to restrain the evil in them. He did not see that his vision of perfection in heart and soul was an ideal toward which humanity must strive with slow upward steps. He was ready to put it all into practice at once. With the eager enthusiasm of his seventeen years, he was ready to be off and reform the world, and he conceived it to be his business to teach the two little girls to help him.

As he talked, the dusk of evening settled over the old churchyard and the curling mists arose like ghostly wraiths from the meadows.

In good time Mr. Timothy Shelley took his son up to Oxford to enter him in the University, and before he left to go back to Field Place, he went to the booksellers with Percy and opened an account for the boy.

"My son," said Mr. Timothy, "is of a literary turn of mind. Should he wish to publish anything, pray indulge him—"

Shelley was delighted with college, and he very soon formed a fast friendship with another freshman named Jefferson Hogg. The two became inseparable. Every morning they went for a long walk during which Shelley behaved like a child, climbing all the banks, jumping all the ditches. When he came to any small body of water he made a little paper boat and launched it on the stream. This was his favorite amusement. Anxiously he watched the fortunes of his tiny bark. Perhaps it was swamped almost at once by winds and waves, perhaps it filled with water gradually and sank. Sometimes, however, it performed its little voyage in safety and reached the opposite shore. Then he was delighted,—it was astonishing how delighted. He would consume all the waste paper he had with him in making these little boats; next he would begin to take the covers of letters, then letters of little value, and finally, after eyeing them wistfully many a time, he would sacrifice the most precious letters of his dearest correspondents, and send them like the others in pursuit of his fairy squadrons down the stream. So long as his paper lasted he would not cease from his sport.

After their walk Hogg and Shelley went up to Shelley's room, where Percy stretched himself out on a rug before the fire and fell fast asleep, curled round upon himself like a cat. By and by he would suddenly start up, rub his eyes with great violence, pass his fingers swiftly through his long hair and enter at once into some vehement argument, or begin to recite verses with an energy almost painful.

Since he hated a regular sit-down meal and hardly ever remained to the end, he kept his pockets always full of bread, dried prunes and pudding raisins. He would walk along, reading and nibbling as he went, and leaving the path behind him marked by a tell-tale line of crumbs.

Now a few days before Christmas Mr. Timothy Shelley found in his letter bag a communication from a London publisher warning him that his son was offering for publication a novel filled with the most dangerous and wicked ideas. The truth was that Percy had seen in his own home and indeed in much of the world about him, the letter of religion with little of its spirit—its form and ceremony with little of its love and sympathy, its tenderness and compassion. Therefore he had jumped to the conclusion that religion itself was to blame for all the bigotry, the lack of love and human kindness in the world, and he, to whom the spirit of love and kindliness meant everything in life, was now busily engaged in pouring out on religion all the phials of his scorn!

Poor Mr. Timothy Shelley! The hen who had hatched a duckling! In great anxiety and with neither imagination nor humor, he prepared to receive his son when he should arrive from Oxford in the way most calculated to bring about the worst results, namely with a long and solemn sermon.

Field Place, which was usually so merry with gay festivities during the holidays, was darkened by these happenings as with a cloud of gloom. Mrs. Shelley advised her daughters not to talk too much with Percy, and the little girls themselves became shy and silent. Christmas preparations were continued as usual, but no one now honestly took any interest in them. There were the same little amusements and surprises of other years, but without the carefree laughter and rollicking fun of a really happy family. Elizabeth, alone, remained faithful to Percy in secret. But her admiration was no longer shared by her cousin, Harriet Grove, who grew colder and colder every day. Indeed, Harriet's papa saw to it that his daughter was quite removed from Percy's contaminating influence by marrying her safely off to a mannerly gentleman, capable of making the best appearance at any county ball. This last blow cut Percy to the heart, for he had dearly loved his cousin.

They wished at Field Place, one and all, except Elizabeth, to mash Percy down, to squeeze him up into that proper mandarin mould which would turn him out capable of bobbing his head one way only, able to say "yes" and never "no" to all the accepted views of his time. They wished to make him a parrot repeating only what they taught him.

"Intolerance! Bigotry!" So said Master Percy. "Obstinate and unreasoning attachment to one's own beliefs and opinions, with no toleration for the beliefs and opinions of others!"

To the fiery youth the black demon of Intolerance seemed to have replaced the fairies and goblins that once haunted the place, and to be stalking in dread darkness through the shadows of hall and park. This demon appeared to the boy the worst he had ever known. No foul fiend, no grizzly Grendel, grim and greedy, fierce and pitiless, man-devouring, ever seemed to the thanes of Hrothgar more terrible than did this dark Spirit of Intolerance to Shelley. He hated it; he longed to do battle with it and wipe it off the earth.

About a month after these unfortunate holidays, Messrs. Munday and Slatter, the Oxford booksellers, with whom Timothy Shelley had opened an account for his son, beheld that young man come bursting into their shop, his hair flying wildly in the wind, his shirt collar wide open, and a huge package of pamphlets under one arm. These pamphlets, he announced, were to be sold at sixpence each, and he wished them prominently displayed in the window of the shop. Indeed, he himself set about arranging them on the counter and in the most conspicuous place in the window in order that none who passed might miss them. The booksellers watched him with an amused and fatherly air, little dreaming of the scandalous title which those pamphlets were flaunting so shamelessly in their decorous front window.

"The Necessity of Atheism!"—That was the name of the pamphlet,—the necessity for believing that there is no God! Had Messrs. Munday and Slatter guessed it, they would have been horrified.

The title, indeed, did not express the young man's real feelings. He had a most ardent belief in a "Spirit of Universal Goodness, the creator and director of all things," he decried only the false and unworthy views of God that made bigots of men. But he liked the word Atheist, it pleased him, it had such a ring of strength, it shocked the intolerant! At Eton the boys had pelted him with the name Atheist. They had flung it at him just as they flung mud. He had felt it to be like a glove of challenge hurled in his teeth. Therefore he had picked it up with defiance to fling it back in the face of that dark demon of Intolerance that lurked in the tyrannical heart of the world.

The Necessity of Atheism had been published but a few minutes when the Reverend John Walker, a Fellow of New College, chanced to pass that way. Wishing to see what was displayed in the window he pressed his nose against the glass. Bang! The glaring letters on the title of that pamphlet fairly slapped the good man in the face,—The Necessity of Atheism!

Astounded and outraged, the Reverend John strode into the shop.

"Mr. Munday! Mr. Slatter!" he called. "What is the meaning of this pamphlet?"

"Really, sir, we know nothing about it," explained the poor shopkeepers, painfully taken aback. "We have not examined it."

"But the title itself is sufficient to have informed you. And now, gentlemen, that your attention has been called to it, you will have the goodness to withdraw immediately every copy from your window and to carry them, as well as any other copies you may possess, into your kitchen and throw them all into the fire."

The upshot of this matter was that a few days later a large official looking document, bearing the college seal, was affixed to the door of the hall. It was signed by the Master and Dean and announced that Percy Bysshe Shelley was publicly expelled from Oxford.

When Mr. Timothy Shelley heard what had happened he fell into a rage and expressed his displeasure by cutting off his son's allowance. Percy himself went up to London in despair. He was alone, without friends, work or money, and tormented by his disgrace.

As long as he lived he never ceased to be astounded at the way the world treated him. He loved the world so ardently, he wanted to make it better, and it was forever kicking him. The fact that he himself had just slapped the world in the face with his Necessity for Atheism did not impress him. He had wanted to wipe out intolerance and bigotry that there might be more love and sweetness in the world. This he had desired because he loved the world, and the world had repaid him by knocking him down. In his misery he passed the time writing melancholy poems or letters to his friend, Jefferson Hogg.

Soon the money question grew serious. Percy was penniless. Fortunately his sisters did not forget him but sent him their pocket money. It was all he had to live on. The girls, all except Elizabeth, were at Mrs. Fenning's Academy for Young Ladies, and Mrs. Fenning's young ladies now had plenty of opportunity to make acquaintance with the fine eyes, the open shirt-collar and tossed curls of Helen Shelley's nineteen-year-old brother.

He would arrive at the Academy, his pockets bulging with biscuits and raisins, and begin an eager discourse on the world's deepest problems to an adoring audience of little girls.

Most of all these girls, Shelley admired his sister's friend, Harriet Westbrook, the daughter of a retired inn-keeper, a lovely child of sixteen with light brown hair and a complexion of milk and roses. When Mrs. Fenning, acting on the orders of Timothy Shelley, requested Percy to visit his sisters less often, Harriet, who often went to her own home in a section of London near Percy's lodgings, would carry to the hermit youth the precious cakes and money entrusted to her by his sisters. Naturally the two young people became the greatest of friends, and Shelley undertook to make over Harriet's mind till it should shine with all the glory of wisdom.

But soon the other young ladies of Mrs. Fenning's Academy began to look askance at Percy. They were influenced by what their elders said. He was a bad boy, a dangerous boy, a boy with very wicked opinions. In good time they began to jeer at Harriet for being the friend of such a youth. With all the cruelty of which girls at that age are capable, they made her miserable with their jeering. After the next holiday, Harriet thought she could not go back to such a school. It was too hard, too terrible. Her father, the stern old inn-keeper, insisted. She should, she must return. In despair Harriet wrote to Shelley. With all the abandon of sixteen years, she declared her case to be desperate. She held herself to be nothing less than an Andromeda about to be delivered by an unfeeling father up to the jaws of the dragon. Shelley saw the case in the same light exactly. Above all things he hated tyranny. Old Mr. Westgrove, he judged, was a tyrant, a terrible old tyrant ready to sacrifice his daughter to the monster of Fenning Academy. He did not hesitate, therefore, to step into the shoes of the hero Perseus and fly to the rescue of the maiden. In a very short time the Edinburgh Mail

Coach was galloping off northward at topmost speed, bearing Perseus and Andromeda away to Scotland to be married.

What would have happened next had not Mr. Timothy Shelley somewhat relented no one knows, but fortunately a friend induced him to thaw out a bit from the icy coldness of his anger and grant Percy a small allowance. Thus the two young things found themselves with enough to live on, at least.

And now great schemes occupied Percy's mind. He would rent a pretty cottage in Wales, perhaps, and establish a House of Meditation to which he would invite only kindred souls who could understand what he and Harriet were driving at, and there they would think out the way to solve all the problems of the world. But before he did this, he would just step over to Ireland and save Ireland from the yoke of British tyranny!

Concerning Ireland, Percy saw the matter with the same clear-cut line of division between the good and the bad, which distinguished all his judgments. Ireland was all right, England was all wrong. Ireland was poor and downtrodden, England was a tyrant. Ireland was a beautiful damsel in distress. He was the Knight Errant who should fly to her rescue ready to fight and die, if need be, in her cause. He fully expected that he would suffer violence for his deeds, martyrdom perhaps. Crowds would follow him in the streets, shouting after him; barbarous English soldiers would seize him, beat him or throw him into prison, but the heroic sweetness of his words would wipe out hatred and work the miracle of reconciling two races that had been foes for centuries. Enwrapped in this rainbow-tinted dream, he was off to the Emerald Isle.

The first thing Shelley did in Dublin was to make an address on Virtue. Instead of expecting their freedom from the British, he said, the Irish should free themselves by becoming sober, just and charitable.

This doctrine Shelley expected would go straight to the heart of the poor Dubliners, and Harriet was no less enthusiastic than he. Their pockets stuffed with copies of this address, the young couple walked up and down the streets, and whenever they met anyone who looked likely to be converted, they slipped a soul-saving paper into his hand, or, from the balcony of their lodgings, they spread the gospel of Virtue by showering pamphlets down on the heads of the passers below. When Shelley shot one skillfully into the hood of an old woman's cloak, Harriet had to run into the house to keep from bursting out into laughter. It was great work saving the Irish, but it was very amusing, too!

Shelley, of course, was constantly expecting to be arrested, but alack! the Irish took all he did with a most annoying composure. The police, indeed, sent a copy of his Address on Virtue to the Secretary of State, but Shelley's advice to the Irish to be sober and tolerant, struck the officials as a screaming joke, and instead of casting the writer into irons, they only enjoyed a round of hearty laughter at his expense.

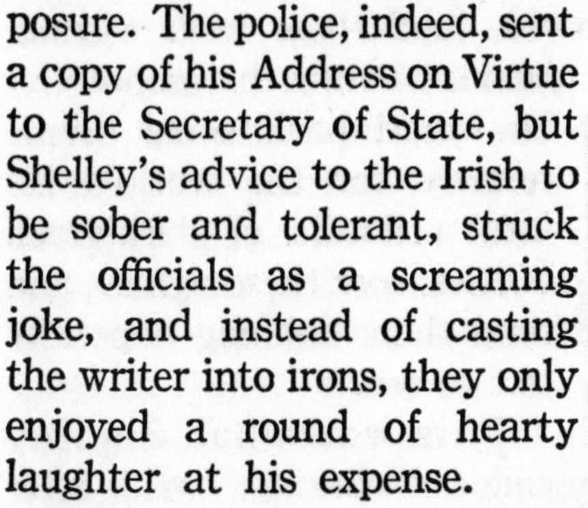

Being thus ignored and left

in security, was very discouraging, and the ways of the Irish themselves were even more so. On St. Patrick's night everybody was drunk and there was a ball at the Castle. Percy and Harriet watched the starving people, far from resenting their poverty, crowd around the state carriages to admire the finery of their tyrants. Such a want of spirit reduced Percy to despair. He and Harriet packed up their remaining pamphlets and went back to England.

From a delightful little cottage with a thatched roof in Lynmouth, however, he did not fail to continue broadcasting his revolutionary ideas by means of pamphlets. When he had written some particularly hair-raising article, he would put it in a box, fit the box out with a mast and sail and launch it on the ocean, or he would make little fire balloons, load these with wisdom and set them sailing into the sky. Again, to vary the monotony, he would pack some divine remedy for the world's ills into a flotilla of dark-green bottles, cork these tightly, and send them bobbing hopefully out to sea.

This was what Shelley called "working," and after he had "worked" hard for a long time, his favorite amusement was to blow soap-bubbles. Pipe in hand, he would seat himself before the door, beneath the climbing roses and myrtles that covered the cottage, and send forth a cloud of shimmering spheres to float airily upward and reflect every changing tint that flitted over the face of earth or sky.

In those days, Shelley's friends began to call him the Elf King, Ariel or Oberon. He was such an unearthly spirit soaring always in the skies; he thought so little of material things, he had such a way of flitting, of being now here, now there, of vanishing just when he seemed certainly chained to some one spot of earth. Moreover, he was just then writing a poem called Queen Mab, wherein he took his flight through silver clouds and starlit sky, all in a magic chariot, drawn by coursers of the air. The name of Ariel suited him perfectly.

Nevertheless, sad days were ahead for Ariel. Earth did all it could to clip his wings. His pretty little child-wife, whose mind he had so carefully made over, began to show herself more interested in bonnets than in philosophy, in shopping than in saving the world. She began seriously to desire not a magic car, but a carriage with horses of flesh and blood, and since the only fairy godmother who could produce such riches was Mr. Timothy Shelley, she began to urge Percy to make up with this angry old fairy in order that he might turn the pumpkin of their poverty into a generous allowance which would permit them to keep a coach, wherein she might drive in state to the dressmaker's and the milliner's.

Shelley was shocked beyond measure at all these worldly considerations. To make up with his father, his wife would have had him do as Mr. Timothy demanded, take back all his opinions and say that he no longer believed what he could not help but believe. To purchase bonnets with such dishonor! To prefer a carriage and horses to independence and upright integrity of mind! Percy was shocked indeed. He himself could get along on the little edge of nothing. His material wants were the fewest, his ideas were bread and meat to him. Save for the fact that he was always needing money to help somebody out of debt or to pay a fine for some too venturesome friend of freedom he had little use for gold. And his Harriet objected, too, to his helping so many people and keeping so little for themselves. Alack! he was woefully disappointed in his pretty little wife.

Matters between the two grew dark. From bad they went to worse till they were completely estranged and separated from one another. Then friends whom Shelley had loved and trusted turned their backs upon him. The very man whom he had loved and honored and helped the most was the harshest in sitting in judgment upon him.

Alack indeed! Ariel began to discover that it was not so easy to turn the world upside down and make it over as he had dreamed in the enthusiasm of sixteen. In these days he often took a boat and rowed among the little islands of the Thames where swans build their nests. Lying at the bottom of his bark, completely hidden by the grasses, he harkened to the "wind in the reeds and the rushes, the bees on the bells of thyme;" he beheld how the "bright clouds float in heaven and dew stars gleam on earth," and at such times he felt, with a thrill of pleasure, that perhaps his real work in life was not to go about like Don Quixote reforming the world, but to seize the beauty of that changing sky, of clouds, and winds and all the fleeting, interweaving harmonies of sun and shade and to fix these in words "light as the lightest leaf that quivers to the passing breeze," yet buoyant as the waterfall that leaps "down the rocks with her rainbow locks, streaming among the streams."

He was still such a boy, this Ariel, and he stood so alone in the world. Few, save his second wife, Mary Godwin, had the courage to take their stand by his side. Together, Percy and Mary went away to Italy, and there they spent all the latter days of Shelley's life, now in Florence, now in Pisa, now in Rome, but forever avoided by the English colonies of the place. True, the headstrong and passionate Lord Byron was Shelley's friend, but a troublesome friend he was, and few others among his countrymen ventured to turn a friendly glance in his direction.

His greatest crime was that he believed in the innate nobility of man. He believed that it was possible for man to rule out the evil in him and be perfect. Such a faith compelled men to recognize their faults and strive toward perfection. It would not leave them comfortable in their sins. The world would have none of him! Yet to the very end Shelley steadfastly upheld his ideals. In his last long poem "Prometheus Unbound," he flung them to the world with a challenge more stirring than any that had gone before.

Shelley was only thirty when he went off to Leghorn in his frail shell of a boat, the Ariel, to meet Leigh Hunt who had just arrived from England. With his usual generosity, Shelley had paid Hunt's passage to Italy, with that of his wife and seven children, and now he was off to see them all safely settled on the lower floor of Lord Byron's palace in Pisa.

When he was ready to return home he set sail from Leghorn on a sultry afternoon that gave promise of a storm. His friends watched his little boat gliding far out to sea until at last she was hid by the haze of the coming mist. That was the last that was heard of Shelley for days! Nearly a week later his body was washed up by the waves on the yellow sands of the bay. The Ariel had foundered in the storm.

"How brutally mistaken men have been about him!" cried Byron beside his body on the shore. "He was without exception the best and least selfish man I ever knew."

Youth, its dreams, its fiery devotion to its ideals, its enthusiasm, its stubborn cry of No Compromise, its absurdity, its glory,—that was the spirit of Shelley.

The Skylark — The Cloud — Arethusa

The Boy of Newstead Abbey

GEORGE GORDON, LORD BYRON (*English*, 1788-1824)

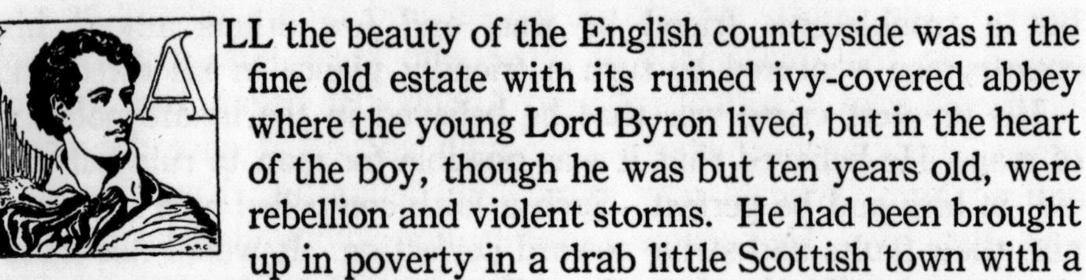

ALL the beauty of the English countryside was in the fine old estate with its ruined ivy-covered abbey where the young Lord Byron lived, but in the heart of the boy, though he was but ten years old, were rebellion and violent storms. He had been brought up in poverty in a drab little Scottish town with a nurse who was cruel and neglectful. They never had money enough; his father had wasted his fortune and that of his wife as well, and then he had gone off and died. A great-uncle at that time owned the family estate and was purposely trying to ruin it out of a fierce dislike for young George Gordon's father and likewise for the boy to whom the lands must go after the uncle died.

No one in the Scottish town thought much of George and his mother, living in their cramped little lodgings. Mrs. Gordon, it was true, claimed descent from the kings of Scotland, but she was high-tempered and queer. She would fall into fits of rage and in a moment of anger might tear a dress to bits. The boy was high-tempered, too, and sensitive to slights and injustice. Moreover, he was lame and too fat. People did not like him much. The girls found other boys far more attractive than he and whenever he opened his heart and poured out affection on some one, his love seemed to meet no return. Shy and lonely, he grew rebellious and unhappy, and, slighted by human beings, he turned his affection to animals, a bear, a wolf or a bulldog.

When he was ten years old the terrible old Lord Byron at last was obliged to die and give up Newstead Abbey. He left George the great estate, ruined, in disrepair and with no sufficient funds to run it. But the spirited new Lord Byron, as he grew to manhood here, determined to wrest from the world some of the things denied him. He would force the world to notice him!

By a course of strenuous exercising, tearing about on horseback with Boatswain, his dog, at his heels, and by still more strenuous dieting, living for weeks at a time on boiled rice soaked in vinegar, the youth got rid of his fat and then suddenly he appeared, to the amazement of those who knew him, a gloriously handsome man, a sort of splendid Apollo. He began, too, writing verses, shocking but arresting thought, and all at once the world noticed him. Women now found him delightful. Even his limp was attractive. He became a literary lion whom all of fashionable London delighted to entertain. But he had longed to pour out love and that had been denied him. Somehow he had grown twisted into a sort of devil, cutting and slashing at life, often cruel to those nearest him and finally he so outraged all public sense of decency that he had to leave England and go to wander and live on the continent.

In the sunshine of Italy Byron found that other rebel, the young English poet, Shelley. The two spent much time together, though Shelley lived in simplicity in the humblest little cottage while Byron dwelt in a palace, fighting his early and painful sense of inferiority with a magnificence of display and a crazy self-assertion which made him do outlandish things.

Having thus wasted his youth, yet feeling the love of freedom the deepest note in his soul, Byron was fired with sympathy in 1823 for the struggling people of Greece who were trying to throw off the yoke of their conquerors, the Turks. Sailing to aid the Greeks, the young man threw himself with deep and fiery devotion into preparations to fight. But before he had been in a battle, he was taken sick and died.

Headstrong, with all his life darkened by his ungoverned passions, Byron was yet a great soul. In the very depths of his heart, it was longing for greater freedom, for some more satisfying love, some larger view of life, some happier state for man, which made him so savage a rebel against the cramped thought of his times.

A Victorian Romance

ELIZABETH BARRETT (1806-1861)
ROBERT BROWNING (1812-1889)

IN a picturesque and lovely home in the Malvern Hills near Wales, there lived once with ten lively brothers and sisters, a little girl named Elizabeth Barrett. The country round about that fine old place was wonderfully green and beautiful:

Dimpled close with hill and valley,
Dappled very close with shade;
Summer snow of apple blossoms
Running up from glade to glade.

And the little girl drank in the loveliness of it all as she raced about, romping with her brothers and sisters. On rainy days when she had to stay indoors, she pressed her face close against the window pane, drawing her little fingers down the long, trailing drops. "Rain, rain, go away, come again another day," said she, and sure enough, the rain would soon disappear and the thrush begin to sing. Then Elizabeth ran out of doors again, chasing along with the sun over hill and dale where the raindrops shimmered on the grass. She was very fond of books, too, that little girl, and when her best loved brother, Edward, began to study Greek with a tutor, she joined him and sat in her little chair with her book in one hand and a doll in the other, persistently twisting her tongue around the strange Greek words. Ever after, Elizabeth loved those old Greek stories and she once had a flowerbed shaped like a giant laid out under the pear tree, where the birds sang in the garden. This giant, she said, was Hector, son of Priam, mighty hero of Troy. He had eyes of blue gentians staring unwinking at the skies, his locks were scented grasses that waved like hair in the breeze; his helmet was daffodils, his breastplate made of daisies; and he bore a sword of lilies. Sometimes Elizabeth said that she dreamed more of these Greek heroes, especially Agamemnon than she did of Moses, her beautiful, little black pony.

The girl was a wonderfully graceful, dainty little creature, with a shower of dark curls falling on either side of a most expressive face. Her eyes were large and tender, richly fringed by dark lashes, and her smile was quick as sunlight.

In childhood her closest chum was her father. Often she used to write poems and show them to him in secret and when she wrote a long poem called *The Battle of Marathon*, her father thought it so fine that he had it really printed in ink.

One day when Elizabeth was fifteen, she decided to go for a ride on her pony, Moses. But Moses was not brought up ready and harnessed exactly on the moment, and so, in a fit of impatience, she flounced out after him into the field. There she attempted to saddle him herself, but as she did so, she fell and the saddle came crashing on top of her. Poor impatient child! She was severely hurt and lay for a long time in bed, and there followed after that, long years of invalidism, during which she never again went out in the old free way, to ramble over the hills and romp in the out-of-doors.

As time passed she lived in various different places, but wherever she went this cloud of illness continuously hung about her. The long days when she was confined to her room, she spent in study and in writing poetry, but for many years she only talked with the outside world by means of letters, — letters always bright and vivacious with little mention of her troubles.

Elizabeth Barrett Browning: My Doves   Hector in the Garden

Gradually the young woman grew to be a well known poet, and then one day a great man, one of the greatest of English poets, wrote Elizabeth Barrett a letter. He admired her, admired her work with all his heart and soul. This man was Robert Browning, and Elizabeth soon admired him as much as he did her. Soon the mail-coach was carrying letters regularly between them. After a time Mr. Browning came to see Elizabeth. She was lying on her sofa helpless when he first came to see her but so great was his vitality, his interest and love for her that almost before she knew it, Elizabeth was married to him and he had carried her off from the prison of her sick room to a beautiful palace in Italy and the golden land of Romance. In her joy and happiness she now found herself transformed and lifted out of her illness.

It was chiefly in the interesting old town of Florence, with its hoary, gray stone buildings and its splendid treasures of art, that the Brownings lived henceforth. Mrs. Browning took the keenest interest in the Italian people who were just then struggling for their independence, and as she looked down on the ardent young patriots from the windows of her home, the famous Casa Guidi palace, she wrote poems full of sympathy for them.

It was in Florence, too, that a little son, Robert, was born, and the mother, who had become the greatest of women-poets, had as much joy in all the wonderful things her little boy did as any less famous mother.

Through many years Elizabeth Barrett and Robert Browning* were remarkably happy together. Perhaps the most outstanding contribution of Mrs. Browning, the first great woman in English poetry, was her plea in *Aurora Leigh* for the intellectual independence of women heretofore almost silent in matters of the mind. Wordsworth had been interested in the living soul of Nature; Keats, in classic beauty; Shelley and Byron, in freedom. Browning was absorbed in human character, in revealing with a startling originality of expression which pointed toward modern poetry, the inner heart and soul of men.

*Robert Browning: *The Pied Piper of Hamelin, An Incident of the French Camp.*

The Little Girl of Griff House

MARY ANN EVANS (GEORGE ELIOT) (*English*, 1819-1880)

ON A bright, frosty morning in old England's picturesque stage-coach days, a little girl and her brother stood before the gate of Griff House, just at the bend of the highroad, waiting eagerly for His Majesty's mail coach to go dashing by. And now they hear the far-off, ringing beat of the horses' hoofs on the ground. Ah! there the great coach comes flashing into view with its four gallant greys at full speed—coachman and guard aloft in scarlet, outside passengers muffled in furs, and baskets and bulky packages dangling merrily at the rear.

That coach was the chief connecting link between Griff and the outside world, and little Mary Ann Evans and her brother, Isaac, watched for it every day; for Griff was a country place in the Midland section of England and far enough from the world it seemed in those days of no railways, no penny post, and no telegraph. Mary Ann's father managed the Arbury estate for its owner, and their home was a charming, red brick, ivy-covered house in the midst of Arbury's pleasant lands. Here, day in and day out, the little brother and sister played. Mary Ann was always at her brother's heels, doing whatever he did. They raced about the old-fashioned garden; they fished in the pond and canal. They peered into the farm offices, the long cow-shed and the broad-shouldered barn; they watched their energetic mother churning the butter and cheese.

An affectionate and impulsive little Maggie Tulliver was Mary Ann, but proud and sensitive to the highest degree, moved easily to either smiles or tears. Moreover, she was too jealously fond of her brother. Her jealous love was painful enough to hurt. She wanted him to love her more than anyone else in the world, and when he was given a pony to which he grew so attached that he

cared but little to play with her, the child was broken-hearted.

Mary Ann had, also, an older sister, Christiana, or "Chrissy," who was always as neat and tidy as Mary Ann was frowsy-haired and wild. Chrissy, because of her neatness, was a great favorite with her three worthy aunts, Mrs. Evans' sisters, who were very like Maggie Tulliver's aunts, the highly superior Dodsons. With these aunts Chrissy used to spend a great deal of time, so that Mary Ann and Isaac were left much alone together. And then came that sorrowful day when the two must be separated, he to go to a boys' school, and she to a girls'. How she looked forward then to the coming of the holidays and how anxious she was when Isaac came home to know all that he had been doing and learning since they parted!

In those days, if one had looked into the Griff dining room on a Saturday night after tea, he would have seen a pretty sight. There in the deep, leather-covered armchair at the right of the ruddy fire-place sits the father, powerful and middle-aged, with strongly-marked features. Between his knees crouches Mary Ann, and he is explaining to her a pretty book of pictures. Her features are strong like her father's, and her rebellious hair is all in her eyes, much to the sorrow of her mother, who sits busily knitting on the opposite side of the fire. Near the mother, all prim and tidy, is the older sister with her work, and between the two groups is the boy, who keeps assuring himself by perpetual search that none of his favorite means of amusement is escaping from his pockets!

Mr. Evans was already very proud of the astonishing intelligence of his little girl. Now, when she came home for the holidays, she and Isaac would devise and act out charades before their aunts and the Griff household, and these were so cleverly done that even the highly superior aunts had to admit their niece of the rebellious hair to be a person of real ability.

From a very early age Mary Ann was accustomed to accompany her father on his drives through the neighborhood. Standing between his knees as he drove leisurely along, she drank in eager impressions of the country and its people. In the Warwickshire of those days they passed rapidly from one phase of English life to another. Now they drove through the countryside with green fields and hedge-rows stretching away as far as the eye could see, and all the people they met were farmers and countryfolk; now they passed a fine old park which shut in some noble mansion house and allowed just a glimpse of its treasure to shine here and there through the trees. Here, they caught sight of grey steeples, pricking the sky, and green and shady churchyards. There, they came on barren land all blackened with coal-pits, and looked down suddenly over a village dingy and dirty with coal dust. Soon they were clattering along on the pavement of a manufac-

turing town. Powerful men they saw here, grimy with coal dust and walking queerly with knees bent outward from long squatting in the mines. These men were going home to throw themselves down in their blackened flannels and sleep through the daylight. In the evening they would rise and spend a good share of their wages at the ale-houses with their fellows. Everywhere were poor cottages and dirty children, and over all could be heard the busy noise of the loom. From windows and doorways peered the pale, eager faces of the handloom weavers, both men and women, haggard with sitting up late at night to finish their toilsome labors. These people made a deep impression on Mary Ann. They had no right to vote, and had long been ground down by the tyranny of their masters. Such towns were often the scene of trades-union meetings and riots. Indeed, when Mary Ann was thirteen years old, she saw one of these riots in the town of Nuneaton. It was the year 1832, when the poorer people, for the very first time, had been given the right to vote for members of Parliament. So eager were they to elect their own candidate and keep out the representative of the wealthier classes, that they formed in a mob threatening and attacking those who wished to vote for their opponents. The magistrate had to call out the Scots Greys to quell the riot, but on the arrival of the soldiers the tumult increased until it assumed alarming proportions. The magistrates themselves were attacked and injured in the very discharge of their duties. Several officers of the Scots Greys were wounded and two or three men, who were attempting to reach the polls, were dragged from the protecting files of soldiers, cruelly beaten and stripped naked. This unhappy outburst of hatred, caused by so many years of oppression, was never forgotten by Mary Ann.

An old-fashioned child she was, living in a world of her own imaginations, impressionable to her finger tips, thinking deeply already, and often at odds with the accepted beliefs of her time. She was full, too, of an eager love for all that was beautiful and longed in her inmost heart to achieve something great, though she often blackly despaired of ever doing anything.

When Mary Ann was sixteen years old her mother died, and soon after this her brother and sister married, so that she became, henceforth, housekeeper and sole companion to her dearly beloved father. As long as he lived she spent the greater part of her time with him in their remote country home. But when he died, she found her way, through the help of friends, out into the greater world. For years, now, she wrote and wrote, translations and articles; but it was not until she was a woman of middle age that she found the work which really made her famous. It was suggested to her then that she write a story, and what should she write about but that old Midland English life which she knew so well and with which she had sympathized so deeply? All at once she found that she could write of men and women so truly and sympathetically that here lay her real life work. Under the name of George Eliot she published a number of novels.

George Eliot was the first English novelist to find all the stirring comedy and tragedy of her books, not in outward events, but in the hearts and souls of men, their inward victories and defeats. And so the little girl of Griff House* wrote *Silas Marner* and *Romola* and became England's greatest woman novelist.

*Mary Anne Evans used the name of a man, George Eliot, because women found it hard to win recognition in literature. Before her there had been only a few women writers such as Jane Austen and Charlotte Brontë.

London Streets

CHARLES DICKENS (*English,* 1812-1870)

IT WAS a crazy, tumble-down old building on the river, the blacking factory where Charles Dickens worked, and it was literally overrun with rats. Charles was only ten years old, shabbily dressed and underfed. He lived in a garret and he had a sausage and a slice of cold pudding for his dinner. Day after day he sat before a little table in the factory and covered pots of blacking with oiled paper, for which work he received the magnificent sum of six shillings a week. Poll Green and Bob Fagin, a rough boy in a ragged apron and paper cap were his companions.

Sometimes, before work began in the morning, Charles would sit on a flight of steps leading down to the Thames and tell stories to a quaint little cockney girl, a slavey who scrubbed floors and washed dishes all day long. Then the dingy warehouses that bordered the river would give way to castles of romance and knights and ladies would cross a bridge of splendor. But when the clock struck, play time was over. The boy went off to his pots of blacking, the girl to her scrubbing, and little did either dream that Charles would some day make that little slavey famous as the "Marchioness" in one of his stories.

Charles Dickens' father was a regular Mr. Micawber, always confidently expecting something to turn up, and always going steadily down in the world. Once he had been a clerk in a navy pay office. There had even been fortunate days when Charles could go to school and read *Robinson Crusoe* and *Don Quixote.* Then for weeks at a time he was not Charles Dickens at all, but one of his heroes. Armed with a broken rod from an old

pair of shoe-trees, he would be Captain Somebody-or-Other of the Royal British Navy and would purchase his life from savages at the cost of a fearful scrimmage. But alack! Mr. Dickens ran into debt and was thrown into a wretched debtors' prison called the Marshalsea. Mrs. Dickens made a forlorn attempt to open a small school and provide for her eight children, but soon the whole family followed the father, and Charles went to work in the factory.

The little fellow felt a bitter sense of neglect and wasted talents. Sometimes, full of fancies and secret ambitions, he would tramp for miles just to look at an elegant red brick house on Gad's Hill, to imagine that it was his and he lived there. After a few years Mr. Dickens inherited enough money to get him out of prison and send his son for a brief time to school. Nevertheless, it was little enough schooling the boy could get. In dark days of grinding toil he would wander, if he had the leisure, through the British Museum to learn what he could by himself.

By the time he was nineteen Charles had fitted himself to be a reporter and, sitting up in the gallery, he reported discussions in Parliament. When he was twenty-five *Pickwick Papers* made him famous. A novelist of the poor before all else was Charles Dickens. What a procession of characters he gives us from the London streets, ludicrous or grotesque, pathetic or lovable. Only those hard days in the blacking factory could have taught him to know these types so well, and his appeal to the hearts of men brought about more than one reform in England in the courts, in the schools, and in wretched debtors' prisons. So at last the little boy was able to buy for his own the elegant house on Gad's Hill.

DAVID COPPERFIELD GREAT EXPECTATIONS OLIVER TWIST A CHRISTMAS CAROL

Watching Vanity Fair Go By

WILLIAM MAKEPEACE THACKERAY (*English*, 1811–1863)

ONCE a small English boy was put on a great sailing ship at the busy wharf of Calcutta to journey from India where he had been born to be educated in England. At the Charterhouse School in London, a rambling, ancient building that looked like a monastery, William Makepeace Thackeray played with the other boys, got in a rough and tumble fight that disfigured his nose for life, pored over his books when he must, and more frequently drew on their pages pictures of Turks and ogres, bandits and highwaymen, or other heroes of favorite tales. It was drawing that interested him more than all the studies in the school.

"Draw us some pictures," the boys would say and straightway William would draw on his slate a funny picture of one of the masters, a master of arts, perhaps, with a head like an ape, a man of letters with a huge hooked nose, or a boy cutting up capers behind a fat official, pompously decked out in the full regalia of his office.

MASTER OF ARTS

MAN OF LETTERS

LIFE AT CHARTERHOUSE GATES

H A L L S   O F   F A M E

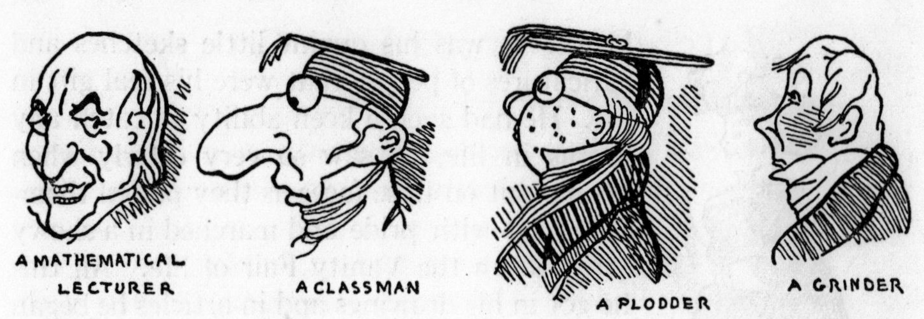

Always Thackeray's pencil was a source of delight to himself and all the other boys. When he grew to manhood, he studied to become a lawyer, but that love of drawing in his heart made him long to be an artist. He would not be satisfied until he had learned to paint. So Thackeray crossed the Channel to France and began to study painting, wandering the narrow lanes of the jumbled Latin Quarter, working in littered studios, where the artists of Paris gathered, and haunting the great picture galleries to copy the paintings there. But though he delighted in painting, he could never really master it; he acquired no skill with the

TRIUMPHAL MARCH

brush. It was his quaint little sketches and caricatures of people that were his real gift in art. He had such a keen ability to catch any shams in life, he saw so very clearly when people put on false faces as they puffed themselves up with pride and marched in a showy array down the Vanity Fair of life. All this he got in his drawings and in articles he began to write for various English newspapers. And one day the rising young author took an English girl as his bride, the wedding being celebrated at the British Embassy in Paris.

The next year after that, Thackeray and his wife returned to live in London where two little daughters were born. And now began his real work as one of England's greatest novelists. Dickens at this same time was writing of London's poor whom he knew so intimately, but Thackeray's life was spent with the rich and aristocratic. He saw all the show and pomp of a fashionable Vanity Fair, marching before his eyes like some gay and gaudy masquerade, and there seemed to him no people more ridiculous on earth than the haughty snobs, all outward appearance and pose with no real worth underneath.

Thackeray made merciless fun of snobs in his books and in articles he wrote for London's funny paper *Punch*. And yet beneath all that show he looked for what he loved most, to find here and there in the crowd some real, simple-hearted gentleman, kindly and sincere, or some wholly sweet-natured woman, unaffected and true.

But just when life seemed serene Thackeray's young wife suddenly became insane and could no longer bear him company. Henceforth his two little daughters were his constant and favorite companions. Now they sat with him in his study helping him make the woodblocks from which to print the quaint drawings with which he illustrated his books. Now they were off with him to visit certain great ladies, showing off with childish delight the costumes they were to wear at Queen Victoria's fancy dress ball. And while he lived here with them he wrote his greatest book *Vanity Fair*, a rich parade of fashionable life in the early days of Queen Victoria.

W.M.T. ON HIS TRAVELS

For a year Thackeray traveled in America delivering lectures there, a tall man of striking appearance with a massive snow-haired head and a sweet smile and gentle manner which endeared him to all who met him. An American, who admired him, honored him with a jingle which well-expressed all that he was.

> *"Ah! blest relief*
> *from pages soft and sacchary,*
> *Give me the writings*
> *of that foe to quackery,*
> *The bold, the keen-eyed,*
> *entertaining Thackeray."*

Thackeray wrote *The Rose and the Ring, Henry Esmond, The Newcomes, Vanity Fair*, and other novels. Somewhat later than Thackeray, Dickens, and George Eliot, were Thomas Hardy and George Meredith, author of *Richard Feverel*. These were the great novelists of the period of Queen Victoria (1837-1901). Charles Kingsley, with his love of the sea; and John Ruskin, with his passion for beauty, lived at this same time, as well as the great Victorian poets. The three greatest periods of English literature were in the reigns of three queens, Elizabeth (1558-1603), Anne (1702-1714), and Victoria (1837-1901). The reign of Edward VII, and George V, in the early 1900's, saw another great group of novelists of whom Joseph Conrad, Arnold Bennett, H. G. Wells, and John Galsworthy were outstanding. To the same period belonged the poets, Rudyard Kipling, Alfred Noyes, and John Masefield with his bounding rhythms of the sea; while in Canada, Bliss Carman was singing in lyric verse.

The Laird of Abbotsford

SIR WALTER SCOTT (*Scotch*, 1771-1832)

UNDER the ruins of an old castle in Scotland a tiny boy once played on the soft green turf among the lambs and dogs. This was little Walter Scott who had been sent down from his home in Edinburgh to his grandfather's farm at Sandyknowe, that he might live out of doors and grow strong, for the child had been lame from his babyhood. Here, under the great shade trees or in a corner of the drawing room, Walter's grandmother and aunt told him endless ballads of Scottish history and tales of the Border heroes. Before he could read he learned these ballads by heart and he loved them so dearly that he would shout them out at the top of his voice, even when the minister came to call, much to the discomfort of that worthy gentleman, who could neither speak nor hear above such a terrific din.

Once Walter's aunt took him to the theatre in London. The play was *As You Like It*, and it all seemed intensely real to the child. When Orlando and Oliver fell to quarreling, he was so grieved that he cried aloud in a voice to be heard throughout the house, "But aren't they brothers?"

As soon as he was strong enough to go to school, Walter became, in spite of his lameness, a leader in frolics and "high jinks." Sometimes he wandered about the country to gather from the peasant folk the quaint old ballads he loved, and he brought away as souvenirs of the different places he visited, the branches of trees from which he eagerly planned to carve a set of chessmen.

"I will make kings and queens from branches growing near palaces," he said, "and bishops from those that have shaded an abbey."

When he said good-bye to school Scott hung out a shingle announcing that he was a lawyer, but his beloved ballads kept running in his head, and so, instead of trying cases, he began to write ballads of his own, *The Lay of the Last Minstrel* and *The Lady of the Lake*. Presently he found himself famous as a poet. Then he bought himself a beautiful home at Abbotsford on the river Tweed, where he lived like a country laird, keeping open house for all visitors amid the gray hills and the heather of the border country that he loved so well.

Here he hoped he should live in peace forever, but he had among his acquaintances a certain swaggering little tailor nick-named Rig-dum-funny-dos. This Rig-dum-funny-dos he placed at the head of a publishing house which he had just organized. But, alack, the little man knew more of cutting a pair of breeches than of running a business, and all too soon he involved his friend in enormous business debts. These must be paid off honorably, and in order to earn the money, Scott plunged at once into work, writing his first novel, *Waverley*. This he published without signing his name to it, and now in an incredibly short time he wrote novel after novel of the splendid Waverley series, calling vividly to life the past of English and Scottish history. Few even guessed that the hospitable Laird of Abbotsford, always surrounded by guests, living in fine old feudal fashion with baronial splendor and hospitality, was the author of these novels. Where did he ever find time to write them? Even the few who knew how early he rose to write, insisted it seemed like magic. "He must keep a goblin," said they, "hidden away in attic or cellar to help him!"

In 1825, after eleven years of brilliant and prosperous labor, he seemed at last about to be free from debt. Just at that very time, however, he found he had been involved again through that publishing business of his, to the huge amount of 130,000 pounds! It was a terrific blow! To pay off this enormous debt, he toiled incessantly once more. Seven years he toiled, a long heroic struggle and in the end his health broke down and he died, but he left a name unstained and held in the highest honor.

Still earlier than the English novelists of Queen Victoria's time was the great Scotch novelist, Sir Walter Scott, who reconstructed vividly the past of English and Scottish history in *Ivanhoe, Waverley, The Talisman, Rob Roy,* and *Guy Mannering.*

The Ploughboy Poet

ROBERT BURNS (*Scotch* 1759–1796)

WILLIAM BURNS might live in a tiny, one-room mud cottage near the town of Ayr in Scotland, but he was a sturdy farmer for a' that, and he meant that Robert and his other children should have an education. So he and four of his neighbors hired a kindly old Scotchman to keep a school for their bairns and they all took turns at boarding him. Little Robert, it is true, liked to play truant from school. He loved each "wee, modest, crimson-tippéd flower," each "cowerin', timorous beastie" of the field far better than his lessons. He loved the "wild, mossy mountains," too, where grouse led their coveys through the heather and shepherds piped while they tended their sheep. Now there was also at this time in the Burns' household an old woman named Betty Davidson, who knew more tales than anyone else in the country concerning fairies, ghosts and devils. In the eerie dusk of the cottage firelight, Robert sat at old Betty's knee and soaked in stories of witches and warlocks, of wrinkled beldames and withered hags, which were later to make a riot of fun through his poem of *Tam o' Shanter*. His mother, too, told him tales of early Scottish history, and many a time he strutted down the village street after the drums and bagpipes, dreaming of Scottish glory. Later, while he followed the

plough he always had some book of old Scotch ballads before him and when the village blacksmith gave him a life of William Wallace, off he must go at once to explore every den and dell where Wallace was said to have hidden.

A sturdy, affectionate lad was Bobbie Burns in those days; but when he grew to be a youth he fell in with evil companions. Certain jovial smugglers who plied their trade in the caves of the rocky Ayrshire coast appealed to him all too well with the lawlessness of their ways. He began to frequent the taverns, to drink and join in their revels. His life went from bad to worse and then his father died leaving a burden of debts; the farm was poor and crops failed, so that Robert found himself tangled in a host of difficulties. The only way out seemed to be for him to leave Scotland and go to seek his fortune in Jamaica.

But for years, as he followed the plough or reaped some golden harvest beside a bonnie lassie, Burns had been writing poetry. Songs came to him as naturally as the carol to the blackbird, songs of the new-turned earth, of lads and lassies of the countryside, or of some wee white cottage where a thrifty wife and her bairns waited to welcome their Dad. So to raise passage money friends now urged the young man to publish some of these poems. The book appeared accordingly and Burns, to his great surprise, found himself grown so popular that instead of going to Jamaica, he was off to Edinburgh to be feted and praised by all.

From the little farm in Ayrshire Burns made his way to the city which towered up proudly before him, picturesque and smoke-wreathed by day, by night a climbing tier of lights. But how could a man like Burns, honestly eager to reverence those who were worthy of honor, endure the standards of the city? How could he see some rich man with scarcely enough ability to make an eight-penny tailor meet with all the fawning notice withheld from a man of genius, merely because he was poor? From the bottom of his heart he wrote:

Is there for honest poverty
That hangs his head and a' that?
The coward slave, we pass him by,
We dare be poor for a' that!
For a' that and a' that,
Our toils obscure and a' that,
The rank is but the guinea stamp;
The man's the gold for a' that!

Ye see yon birkie called a lord,
Wha struts and stares and a' that;
Though hundreds worship at his word,
He's but a coof for a' that.
For a' that and a' that,
His ribband, star, and a' that,
The man of independent mind,
He looks and laughs at a' that.

In the very heyday of his success in Edinburgh, Burns began to see that he should have to return to the country, don his "hodden-grey" once again and follow the plough. So, he turned his back on the city, married a country lassie, and settled down to a small farm at Ellisland, with high hopes that here he should be happy. But poor Burns! In spite of his warm heart and love of laughter, he yielded too easily to temptation ever to be happy. The taverns and ale-houses saw him frequently again. How then could he make Ellisland pay? In a short time he had to sell it. With his wife and children he moved into the drab little town of Dumfries. Now he was separated from all that rustic country life and picturesque, rural scenery that had been his inspiration. He turned down no more daisies in the field; the horned moon hung no longer in his window pane. Amid the dirty streets, the gossip and dissipation of a third-rate Scottish town, he was neither in harmony with himself nor with the world. And so, at the age of thirty-seven, worn out and old before his time, the greatest poet of Scotland died.

Robert Burns, in Scotland, lived at the same time as the English poet, William Blake, but he stood alone as a poet of his day, thoroughly Scotch in his spontaneous singing of life's simple joys and sorrows. Well-known poems are *Tam O'Shanter, To a Mountain Daisy, The Cotter's Saturday Night,* and *For A' That.*

A Rover in the Catskills

WASHINGTON IRVING (*American*, 1783-1859)

LONG, long ago, just at the close of the American Revolution, when New York was a little old town with all the air of an overgrown village, a small boy was born there whose mother named him Washington Irving in honor of General Washington. When the little fellow was about six years old his nurse took him one day to see the procession escorting General Washington to Federal Hall to take his oath as first President of the United States. Pressing through the throng, the nurse dragged her small charge up to the great man and told him that the boy had been given his name. With a kindly smile Washington stopped to give his young namesake his blessing.

Washington Irving grew to be an adventurous lad. He liked to visit new scenes and observe strange manners and customs. When he was still the merest slip of a child he made long tours of discovery into foreign parts, the foreign parts of his own little city, and more than once his parents had to employ the town-crier to hunt up their wandering son by crying his name through the town. He loved to roam around the Battery, and to wander out on the piers to watch the out-going ships departing to distant climes. With what longing eyes did he gaze after their lessening sails and waft himself in fancy to the very ends of the earth. As he grew into boyhood, Washington extended the range of his adventures. He now spent his holiday afternoons in rambles far out into the country round about New York, visiting the little villages where the descendants of the old Dutch settlers continued to dwell, and pushing on, on to the very distant hills. He made voyages, too, in a sail-boat up the lordly Hudson River whose

Irving was the first great figure in American letters. Before his time, the New World had produced no writer of note. Intensely American in spirit, he still wrote in the style of English authors preceding Queen Victoria.

cliffs and towering highlands breathed forth the very spirit of old Dutch and Indian legends. He penetrated into the heart of the Catskill Mountains, that rise to the west of the river, changing their magical hues with every hour of the day.

At times he peered into some dark glen, lonely and wild and tangled, or stood at the foot of a waterfall, a sliding sheet of silver, slipping down over mossy rocks; again he came out on the edge of a precipice, whence he could look out for miles and miles over all the sun-flooded valley and see far down below the twisting ribbon of the Hudson. He knew those mountains in sunshine and in storm—now in the calm of evening when they threw their long blue shadows peacefully over the valleys, or gathered a hood of gray vapors about their heads to glow in the setting sun like a crown of glory—now when the thunderclouds lowered, the lightning went leaping from crag to crag and peal after peal of thunder rolled crashing down their heights. And at the foot of these fairy mountains, its smoke curling up through the trees, would nestle a little Dutch village, where the houses had latticed windows and the gable fronts were surmounted by the quaintest of weathercocks. Here in the shade of some great tree before the old tavern, Irving

could always find a club of worthies smoking their pipes and whiling away the long, lazy summer's day by telling endless stories.

But as the boy grew to young manhood, he began to long to go further still in his travels. He had seen and loved so much of the natural beauty of America, her mighty lakes and mountains, her valleys and trackless forests, her broad, deep rivers and boundless plains, but now old Europe beckoned him. He longed for her treasures of art, her quaint and different customs, her poetic associations. He longed to loiter about her ruinous old castles, and reconstruct in his fancy all the shadowy grandeur of her past. And so when the young maid who had been his sweetheart died and there was nothing more to hold him in America, off he went to England. Already he was known there as the author of *Salmagundi Papers* and that humorous mixture of fact and fancy, *Knickerbocker's History of New York.* And so in England he found a place ready made for him. He could travel now as much as he pleased and he set down in his *Sketch Book* all the interesting things he saw—little home scenes of rural repose and sheltered quiet, peasants in country lanes, as well as the solemn magnificence of grand old Westminster Abbey.

A journey to Spain gave him the rich store of Spanish and Moorish legend to put into *The Alhambra* and *The Conquest of Granada.*

After seventeen long years abroad, Irving returned to New York and bought the beautiful place called Sunnyside at Tarrytown on the Hudson, not far from Sleepy Hollow. No woman ever replaced the sweetheart of his youth and Irving never married, but here at beautiful Sunnyside he passed all the rest of his days, quitting it only once for any length of time, and then to serve for four years as American Minister to Spain. But however great was the volume of work that Washington Irving put forth, his name always calls first to mind the magic of the Catskills and the Hudson, gleaming through mists of romantic old Dutch legends.

THE LEGEND OF SLEEPY HOLLOW — RIP VAN WINKLE

The Father of American Song

WILLIAM CULLEN BRYANT (*American*, 1794-1878)

ONE of the descendants of that arch little Puritan maiden, Priscilla Mullins, and her bashful lover, John Alden, was a small boy named William Cullen Bryant. William was born in the beautiful hilly country of Cummington, Massachusetts, fit cradle for a real poet of Nature. His father, Dr. Peter Bryant, was a country physician, and he used to love to wander with his sons out into the wild woodlands and up into the hills, keen-eyed and alert to each flash of little woodland creatures through the leaves, loving them all and lifting up his heart with joy for all Nature's ways of beauty. In the long winter nights, when the snow lay white on the world without and a roaring fire blazed on the cosy hearth within, Dr. Bryant would read aloud to his children from the treasures of his library which was one of the largest in the neighborhood. During the day the boys went to the public school, but when the school hours were over they raced out into the woods and fields, exploring all the country round about.

When Cullen grew to young manhood he was sent to Williams College, but his father was too poor to permit him to finish his education at Yale University, as he had hoped, and so for a time he pursued his studies at home. It was at this period, when he was still little more than a youth, that, as he was one day wandering in the forest, his thoughts framed themselves into *Thanatopsis*.

> *To him who in the love of nature holds*
> *Communion with her visible forms, she speaks*
> *A various language:*

Having written the poem down on paper he laid it aside and forgot it altogether. It was not until some six years later that his father accidentally discovered it, took it to Boston and had it published. It produced a decided impression at once, for no American poet had yet written anything to equal it.

From this time forth, though Cullen had been educated for a lawyer, he continued to devote himself to literature. In 1825, he became editor-in-chief and part proprietor of the New York Evening Post, a position which he held for fifty years.

When the question of the abolition of slavery began to be agitated, Bryant in the Post, took the side of the Abolitionists. This stand was decidedly unpopular in those days and brought down upon it a storm of abuse. Mr. Bryant, however, refused to surrender his convictions, although he was denounced and deserted by many of his former friends, and was more than once threatened by the violence of the mob.

In 1860 he was one of the presidential electors who chose President Lincoln, and ever afterward he enjoyed the confidence and friendship of Lincoln. During the dark days of the Civil War, when all too many deserted and betrayed that gaunt, lone man in the President's chair, Bryant stood firmly by him, ever aiding and supporting him; and no other journal was more instrumental than the Post in bringing about the great changes of public opinion which ended in the destruction of slavery.

Mr. Bryant lived to be a very old man. He was the first American poet to win permanent distinction and he exercised a mighty influence over the younger literary men of America.

Poems by Bryant are *Thanatopsis*, and *To A Waterfowl*. While Bryant was writing, James Fenimore Cooper (1789-1851) was portraying the romance of the frontier and Indian life in *Leather Stocking Tales*.

A Young Quaker of New England

JOHN GREENLEAF WHITTIER (*American*, 1807-1892)

IT WAS cold in Haverhill in the winter. Sometimes the Whittier family was snowbound for days, but the house was cheery and homey with its blazing fire, and the snow without made a world of fairy beauty. John was the son of a hard-working, deeply religious Quaker family, and his days were spent in work, in quiet home joys and in husky out-of-door sports. Once he made a trip to Boston. What an event it was! With what expectation did he look forward to it, and how the whole household lent itself to furthering so great an expedition! He was not only to have a new suit of clothes, but they were, for the first time, to be trimmed with "boughten buttons," a clear mark of distinction, to the boy's way of thinking, between town and country fashion. In his fresh homespun clothes, cut after the best usage of the Society of Friends, he started bravely by the coach to pass a week with a relation, Mrs. Greene, in Boston.

Mrs. Greene greeted him with affectionate hospitality, and he sallied forth at once to the great business of seeing the sights. Up and down he wandered, up and down, but, alack, how bewildering did the streets appear! Somehow it wasn't at all as he had expected. The crowd grew worse and worse, thicker and thicker, more intent on jostling and pushing. Such a terrible stream of people! And they paid no heed to him whatever. He began to think his new clothes and his buttons were thrown away. Suddenly he felt very homesick. To these city folk it made no difference at all about his "boughten buttons." Sadly he went back to Mrs. Greene's to drink a cup of tea, but there he found a gay company gathered, who begged him to go to the theatre. This suggestion thoroughly shocked his careful Quaker training and completed his misery. With all his heart he longed to be at home.

John was always writing poetry which he hid from everyone but his sister Mary. One day he was helping his father to mend a fence when the postman, passing his gate, tossed him a newspaper and what should he see but one of his own verses in print! He could scarcely believe his eyes! His sister had secretly sent the poem to the *Free Press*, a paper published by that bold and sturdy foe to slavery, William Lloyd Garrison. Not long afterward Garrison came to see the poet while he was working in the cornfield and urged his father to send him to some higher school. Mr. Whittier had not the money for the purpose, but someone offered to teach the youth to make ladies' shoes and slippers during the winter. Thus he put himself through two years at Haverhill Academy.

Whittier became, in time, the great poet of the anti-slavery movement and a writer of beautiful hymns still sung in churches today; but he was, first of all, the poet of New England farm life. He sang of corn and pumpkins and barefoot boys, of corn-huskings, of the homecoming of all the family at Thanksgiving, and the world of New England snows, with cozy life indoors.

The Barefoot Boy, Barbara Frietchie, Maud Muller, In Schooldays.

The Lonely Boy

NATHANIEL HAWTHORNE (*American*, 1804-1864)

THE solitary figure of a boy, alone on a rocky cliff overlooking the sea at Salem. The surge beating up on the shore and the vast ocean stretching away before him. How Nathaniel loved the sea! His father had been a sailor and sailed far away to the Indies, to Africa and Brazil. Sometimes Nathaniel said to his mother that he, too, would go to sea and never come back again. A shy, solitary lad was he, fond of his own fancies, and of long, lonely rambles along the shore or through the queer little streets of Salem with their quaint old doorways and tragic memories of early witchcraft days.

When Nathaniel was fourteen his mother moved to a little town in Maine on the fresh, bright waters of Sebago Lake. Here the lad began again his solitary walks. He roamed the woods by day with his gun and rod, and in the moonlight nights of winter, he skated upon the lake till midnight, alone, always alone. When he found himself far from home and wearied with exercise, he often took refuge in some wood-cutter's cabin, where half a tree would be burning upon the hearth.

But when Nathaniel grew up, he did not go to sea. He went to Bowdoin College, instead, where he met two interesting youths, Franklin Pierce and Henry Wadsworth Longfellow. While he was here certain new desires took root in his heart, for he wrote to his mother, "How would you like some day to see a whole shelf full of books written by your son, with '*Hawthorne's Works*' printed on their backs?"

When he was graduated from Bowdoin, instead of making off to sniff salt whiffs of old Ocean from behind the mast, he returned to Salem, and took to writing, living in such seclusion that even his own fellow citizens scarcely knew him by sight!

Little money, however, came from his magazine articles, and all too soon, life unrolled another picture,—Nathaniel now a weigher in the Customs House at Boston, measuring coal, salt and other bulky commodities that came in on foreign vessels. Thereafter, Nathaniel doing a farm hand's chores at Brook Farm, striving with other earnest thinkers, to work out a way for men to lead better and simpler lives.

In 1842 Hawthorne married and settled down in the handsome Old Manse at Concord. A beautiful place it was and all his rich life there called forth a book which he named with tender affection *Mosses from an Old Manse.*

In the years that followed Hawthorne lived for a time in a little red wooden house at Lenox in the Berkshires where he led an idyllic life of peace, happy in the companionship of his wife and their three children. Their home stood in the midst of a broad valley that was like a great bowl flooded with golden sunshine. In the center there was a lake and all around an amphitheatre of hills about whose quiet peaks hung delicate purple mists like the softest of airy veils. Here Mr. Hawthorne would lie in the sunshine flecked with the shadows from a tree, and his little Una, Rose and Julian would climb over him and cover his chin and breast with grass till he looked like Pan, the merry god of the woods, with a verdant woodland beard. With children he was always happy and he loved to tell them stories.

In 1853 Hawthorne's college friend, now President Pierce, sent him to Liverpool as American Consul and for seven years he remained abroad. When he returned once more to America, he went to live in Concord, where he knew Louisa Alcott, Ralph Waldo Emerson, Henry Thoreau and all the other interesting Concord people. In that lovely spot he spent the rest of his days.

Life in Concord

LOUISA MAY ALCOTT (*American*, 1833–1888)

IN THE historic old town of Concord, Massachusetts, there lived once a strong, sturdy, jolly girl named Louisa Alcott. Louisa's home was a shabby, dingy old house, but it was full of merry laughter for Louisa had a good mother, a devoted father, and three lively sisters, Anna, Beth, and May. Over the hills behind Old Concord and down by the rush-bordered river that meandered through the town, the little girls romped and played.

They weren't very well off so far as money goes, for Mr. Alcott was a schoolteacher with very peculiar ideas as to how children ought to be taught, so all too often he couldn't get pupils enough to keep his family well-fed. In days when the birch rod, well-applied to a naughty boy, was highly thought of as discipline, Bronson Alcott flogged himself to punish an unruly child! Moreover, he took children walking, swimming, and rowing; he showed them the world around them instead of keeping their noses always glued to their books. Such methods did not make him popular. That was no way to teach children, grown-up people said.

From his earliest days, Bronson Alcott had been a dreamer. As a young man, he had traveled as a peddler with the tin trunk in his wagon full of Yankee notions, pins, scissors, combs, thimbles, puzzles, and what-not; and always as he traveled, he looked for some school where he might be able to stop and exercise his ideas.

Moreover, this strange young man believed and earnestly preached that people should lead simpler, truer, more useful lives than they do and his opinions as to how they should set about doing this were so different from those held by others, that people made fun of him generally. They said he was odd and called him a crank.

"He's bent on saving the world by a return to acorns and the Golden Age!" one man said.

"But no man can laugh at him without loving him," the same man added.

So Louisa's father went about Concord with his mild eyes radiant, working by the day for his neighbors, chopping their wood, digging gardens, and laboring like a farmhand, to provide food for his family when he didn't have pupils enough.

At least the Alcotts had plenty of apples. A basket of golden russets always stood on the table. Usually there was also bread, potatoes, and boiled rice with grated cheese when the family sat down to dinner.

True, when Mrs. Alcott's cousins came for a visit, they had to bring their own tea and pepper, for the Alcott's rarely had such expensive trimmings on their table. As soon as they were able to provide rice and turnips for themselves, they were sure to cut their meals down to two a day in order to share what they had with some neighbor who had a drunken husband or was otherwise in trouble.

But Concord was a better place for Bronson Alcott to live than the city of Boston had been where the family had lived before, for there were other people in Concord, whom the world might, perhaps, call queer.

There was Ralph Waldo Emerson, poet and philosopher, writing his essays on Love and Friendship and dreaming of life in the spirit. There was that strange man, Henry Thoreau, who went off and lived alone for two years in a hut on Walden Pond, just to prove to himself and others the joys of simple living close to the heart of Nature. And there was Nathaniel Hawthorne, earnestly pondering like old Puritans of Pilgrim days, the problems of right and wrong and writing of the stern punishments that overtook evildoers. All these men loved Louisa's father and held him in high esteem.

Shoulder to shoulder with Bronson Alcott stood his wife, always upholding him, working day and night with her capable hands to make his burdens lighter, cooking, sewing, cleaning. And in spite of all the hard work she did, she was never too tired to be gay and jolly and interested in all that interested her daughters. So the four little girls were brought up from their infancy in a world of simple living and high thinking. They had plenty of joyous, carefree fun in which both mother and father joined, but they began to understand very early the necessity for being useful and bearing their share in the household tasks. Thus, though the house where they lived was poor and shabby, it was very rich in love and loyalty and simple homey joys.

Louisa was a strong, active, handsome girl with blue eyes and a perfect mane of heavy chestnut hair. She could run for miles and miles and never get tired and she was as sturdy as a boy. Indeed, her mother used sometimes to call her Jo in fun and say that Jo was her only son. Jo loved to climb trees and leap fences, run races and roll hoops, and when she was not playing with her sisters she liked best to play with boys. But beside all these lively sports, Louisa liked, too, to curl herself up in a chair and read or study. Sometimes she would go off alone into the garret, taking a pile of apples with her and her favorite book. There she would read and munch away in happy solitude. All day long she had interesting thoughts and often she made up stories with which she held her sisters spellbound.

On occasion, little Louisa could be a turbulent miss and her high spirits often led her into paths of strange adventure. Once, when she was very small and lived in Boston, she ran away from home and spent the day with some Irish children. They shared a very poor and very salty dinner with her, after which they all went to play in the nice, dirty, ash heaps. Late in the afternoon they took a daring trip as far away as Boston Common. When it began to grow dark, however, Louisa's little Irish friends deserted her, and there she was left all alone in a strange place with the dusky shadows deepening and the night lights twinkling out. Then, indeed, she began to long for home, but she hadn't the smallest idea which way to go and so wandered helplessly on and on. At last, quite wearied out, she sat down on a welcome doorstep beside a friendly big dog. The dog kindly allowed her to use his back for a pillow and she fell fast asleep. From her dreams, she was roused by the voice of the town crier who had been sent in search of her by her distracted parents. He was ringing his bell and calling out loudly:

"Lost! Lost! A little girl six years old, in a pink frock, white hat, and new green shoes!"

Out of the darkness a small voice answered, "Why dat's me!"

Next day the little runaway was tied to the arm of a sofa to cure her of her wandering habit. But, whenever Louisa was naughty, she was always terribly sorry and pondered over her sins in a way that would have done credit to Nathaniel Hawthorne, himself, pondering with tense moral earnestness over the sins of the world. In the intervals of working off steam in the liveliest adventures, she worried over her faults. Sometimes, then, she had a little game she played. She made believe that she was a princess and that her kingdom was her own mind. When she had hateful or self-willed thoughts, she tried to get rid of these by playing that they were enemies of her kingdom. She would marshal her legions of soldiers and march them against the foe. Her soldiers, she said, were Patience, Duty, and Love. With these she fought her battles and drove out the enemy. When she was only fourteen years old, she wrote a poem about this:

A little kingdom I possess,
Where thoughts and feelings dwell,
And very hard I find the task
Of governing it well.

Nevertheless, after many a hotly contested battle, she did succeed in taking command and governing her kingdom like a queen.

The house where the four girls lived in Concord had a yard full of fine old trees and a big barn which was their most particular delight. Here they produced many marvelous plays, for Anna and Louisa both had a wonderful talent for acting. They made the barn into a theatre and climbed up on the haymow for a stage, while the grown people who came to see their plays sat on chairs on the floor. One of the children's favorite plays was Jack and the Beanstalk. They had a ladder from the floor to the loft, and all the way up the ladder they tied a squash vine to look like the wonderful beanstalk. When it came to the place in the story where Jack was fleeing from the giant and the giant was hot on his heels, about to plunge down the beanstalk, the girl who took the part of Jack would cut down the vine with a mighty flourish while the audience held their breath. Then, crashing out of the loft to his well-deserved end below, came the monstrous old giant. This giant was made of pillows dressed in a suit of funny old clothes, with a fierce, hideous head made of paper.

Another play which the children acted was Cinderella. They made a big pumpkin out of the wheelbarrow trimmed with yellow paper. Thus the pumpkin could easily become a golden coach in which Cinderella magnificently rolled away at a single stroke of the fairy godmother's wand. The tale of the foolish woman who wasted her three wishes was illustrated in a way to make the beholders scream with laughter, by means of a pudding which was lowered by invisible hands until it rested upon the poor lady's nose.

The costumes used in these performances were marvelous affairs; for Louisa, Anna and Mrs. Alcott had a wonderful knack for rigging up something out of nothing. A scrap found its use. A bright colored scarf, a table cover, a bit of old lace, a long cloak, a big hat with a plume stolen from some departed bonnet, would afford a regal costume in which to come sweeping on the stage. Furthermore, the children were never at a lack for scenery; for their ready wit was quite capable of providing castles, enchanted forests, caves or ladies' bowers, and barns offered splendid opportunities for a hero or a villain to make desperate but

safe leaps from the beams, or to sink out of sight at short notice.

There was one other beautiful and much more serious story which the Alcott children loved to play, though they did not give this to an audience in the barn, but played it alone for their own amusement. This story was Pilgrim's Progress, in which the pilgrim, Christian, loaded down with his burden of sins, finds his way through toil and danger from the City of Destruction to the Celestial City. Their mother used to tie her piece-bags on their backs to represent Christian's burden. Then they would put on broad-brimmed, pilgrim hats, take a stick for a staff and start out on their journey. From the cellar, which was the City of Destruction, they mounted to the housetop where was the Celestial City, and they acted out on the way, in most dramatic form, every step of Christian's upward progress. Sometimes, instead of playing Pilgrim's Progress indoors, they played it out of doors, wandering over the hills behind the house, through the woods and down the lanes.

There could not have been a more beautiful place than Concord for four hearty, simple girls like these to live. It was a typical New England village, quiet and homelike, with its plain, white houses and its shady elm trees, nestling in its circle of peaceful hills. There were no very rich people there and none very poor. The inhabitants were honest and friendly, with simple occupations and amusements and very few worldly ambitions. In the winter the place rang with the happy voices of young people skating on the hardened snow in the pine woods. In the summer the river was alive with gay bathing or boating parties.

Concord was an historic old place, too, with its memories of the first gun-shots of the Revolution, and many a time in the days of the Alcott girls, there were masquerades on the river to celebrate the anniversary of that great event. Gay barges full of historic characters in costume glided down the stream, and sometimes savages in their war paint darted from the lily-fringed river banks to attack the gay masqueraders. Hearty and healthy was the life in Concord, and it produced a fine race of people, among them three, at least, of most remarkable character. These three were Emerson, Hawthorne, and Thoreau, the friends of Louisa's father, who belonged to the great New England group of writers, the most distinguished local group America has ever produced.

Ralph Waldo Emerson, living in the big white house on the turnpike, was a thinker, philosopher, and poet, strong, gentle, and serene. He had stood by Mr. Alcott when everybody else laughed at him and deserted him, and, from her earliest recollections, Louisa had adored him. Once she went to school with the little Emersons in their father's barn; for, in those days of no public schools, teachers used frequently to gather their pupils together in barns. The illustrious Mr. Emerson was often the children's playfellow. He would pile all the youngsters on a haycart and take them off to picnic or go berrying in the woods.

The favorite place for such picnics was the hut which Emerson's friend, Thoreau, had built on the edge of Walden Pond when he wanted to retire from the world. This hut stood in a beautiful spot among the fragrant pines and it overlooked the clear, green depths of the water, which Thoreau, from its gleaming expressiveness, called the "Eye of the Earth." All about rose tall, green hills and around the pond, through the woods, there ran an old Indian trail which had been worn hard through the centuries when the red men tramped over it on the hunt. When they came to this beautiful spot, Emerson showed the children all the places he loved; all the wood people Thoreau had introduced to him; or the wild flowers whose hidden homes he, himself, had discovered. So, years later, when the children read Emerson's beautiful poem about the sweet rhodora in the woods, his "burly, dozing bumblebee," or his fable of the Mountain and the Squirrel, they recognized old friends of these beautiful woodland jaunts.

To the turbulent, restless, half-grown Louisa the calm philosopher, with his gentle ways and practical common-sense, was an anchor indeed. In her warm little heart he was held so sacredly that he himself would have smiled at such worship. She went to him often for advice about her reading, and was at liberty to roam all around the book-lined walls of his library, there to select whatever pleased her most; for Emerson was never too busy to help her.

Hawthorne, too, handsome, shy man that he was, always steering away from the society of grown-ups, had much to do with Louisa and the Concord children. He was always at his best with children, and his stories never failed to hold Louisa spellbound. Doubtless she was one of the children to whom he first told the *Tanglewood Tales* and the stories in the *Wonder Book.* She pored over his books, and love and admiration for him grew with her growth.

Henry Thoreau was the last of those great Concord friends who had such an influence on Louisa's life. From him the Alcott

girls learned to know intimately the nature they already loved, and many a happy day was spent with him in the woods, studying the secrets of the wildflowers and the language of the birds. It was down by the river that Thoreau was most often to be found. There he would row his boat or paddle his canoe with Indian skill through the many windings, stopping now and then to gather some rare plant from among the grasses on the shore. In his company the girls took long, long walks, even tramping the twenty miles from Concord to Boston. There was not a single flower or tree that the gentle woodsman did not know; birds, squirrels and insects were his comrades. Hunted foxes would come to him for protection; wild squirrels would nestle in his coat; birds and chipmunks gathered about him as he sat at rest on the river bank; he seemed able even to coax the fishes up to the surface to feed out of his hand. And so for him all Nature had a voice, and the Concord children loved the simple friend who taught them the poetry of the woods.

As Louisa grew up into a tall young girl she began to come into prominence as a story teller. Her nature studies gave her material, and out in the Concord woods she would gather about her the little Emerson children, Ellen, Edith and Edward, and the three Hawthorne children, Una, Julian and Rose, and many another, too. Then, under the spreading branches of some great tree, with the sunshine filtering down on her head and lighting up all the eager little faces about her, she would tell stories that made the very woods alive—wood-sprites and water-sprites and fairy queens dancing in and out through the greenery of those cool forest glades.

But in spite of all the delights of Concord, Louisa was beginning to feel the weight of the family troubles. She saw her father struggling day by day, earning a little here and there by the work of his hands when his talents as a teacher were running to waste. She saw her mother carrying burdens too heavy for her and working far too hard. She had always helped her mother as much as she could with the housework, but the greatest need of the household now was for money. A splendid purpose took root in Louisa's heart. She would set out into the world, earn a living, and mend the family fortunes. She would give this dear devoted mother the comforts that had been denied her so long.

Once determined to accomplish this, Louisa never rested. True, she was only a girl, and there were very few lines of activity open to girls in those days. The way seemed dark before her and full of obstacles. But Louisa was never daunted. Full of energy and pluck, she set forth. First she went up to Boston and lived in a wretched little sky-parlor. There she wrote stories for various magazines and papers, taught in a kindergarten and did sewing or anything else that came to her hand. Only one thing mattered to her henceforth, to help her mother, father and sisters. Night and day she worked, never sparing herself, and every penny that she did not absolutely need for the barest necessities of life, she sent home to her mother and father. James Russell Lowell was the editor of the *Atlantic Monthly* in those days and he praised her stories and took them for his magazine. Yet, as the years passed, she wrote nothing that had any very lasting merit. She merely labored unceasingly and earned money enough by her own self-sacrifice to keep her dear ones in greater comfort at home.

Then one day Louisa's publisher asked her to write a book for girls. Louisa was very worn and weary, and she hadn't the smallest idea that she could really write an interesting book for children. All these years she had written for grown-ups only. But she had never yet said, "I can't" when she was asked to do anything. So in spite of her misgiving she answered the publishers simply, "I'll try."

When she began to think about what she should write, Louisa remembered all the good times she used to have with her sisters in the big, bare house in Concord, out in the old barn, and over the hills. So she began to write the story of *Little Women* and to put in all those things. Besides the jolly times and the plays they had, she put in the sad, hard times too, the work and the worry and the going without things. It was a simple story of simple girls, of their daily struggles, their joys and sorrows, but through it all shone the spirit of that beautiful family affection that the Alcotts knew so well, an affection so strong and enduring that neither poverty, sorrow, nor death could ever mar it. And the little book was so sweet and funny, so sad and real, like human life, that everybody bought it and it brought in a great deal of money for Louisa.

There were Mr. and Mrs. March in the book, true as life to Mr. and Mrs. Alcott, and there were all the four sisters, too. Meg, the capable house-wifely one, was Anna; Jo (the old pet name for Louisa) was Louisa, herself, the turbulent, boyish one, who was always "going into a vortex" and writing stories; Beth was the sweet, sunny little home-body, Lizzie or Beth; Amy was May, the pretty, golden-haired, blue-eyed one, with the artistic tastes, whose pug nose was such a sore trial to her beauty-loving soul that she went about with a clothespin on it to train it into proper lines. There was a real John Brooke, too. He was a portrait of that gentle, kindly, lovable John Pratt, who really married Anna. And Laurie was a mixture in whom Louisa combined a handsome Polish boy she once met in Europe, with a certain New England lad who was her friend in girlhood. So, many of the good times in *Little Women* are true, and many of the sad times, too—the marriage of Meg and John Brooke, and the death of little Beth.

Louisa was hardly prepared for the immense success of this book. It made her almost rich; and, besides that, she suddenly found herself so worshipped and idolized by young people and old alike that crowds began haunting her path, hanging about the house to get just a glimpse of her, popping up in her way to bow reverently as she went for a walk or a drive, deluging her with flowers, and writing her sentimental verses.

All this attention drove Louisa nearly distracted, so she had to run away from it for a year's rest in Europe. But, ever after that, the children considered Louisa their especial property and she devoted herself henceforth to writing for them entirely. She loved them very dearly, too, boys and girls alike; and no American author has ever held a warmer place than she in the hearts of American young people.

Thus, after so many years of hard and devoted labor, Louisa's dream came true. She was able to give her family all they needed and wanted. She bought a comfortable home for them in Concord, she sent May to study art in Europe, she gave her father books; but, best of all, she was able at last to give her beloved mother the happiness and rest which she had so nobly earned. Never again did "Marmee" have to do any hard work. She could sit from that time forth in a comfortable chair beside the sunny window, with beautiful work and beautiful things about her.

Through endless toil and effort, Louisa's life ended in success and it had been her privilege to live much of it in company with the greatest group of literary men America ever produced.

Read the *Life of Louisa May Alcott*, by Belle Moses,
and Miss Alcott's own books:
Little Women *Little Men* *Jo's Boys* *An Old-Fashioned Girl* *Rose in Bloom* *Jack and Jill*
Eight Cousins *Silver Pitchers*

The Harvard Professor

HENRY WADSWORTH LONGFELLOW (*American*, 1807–1882)

ACROSS the Charles River, from Boston, and some twenty miles from Concord, lay the quiet old city of Cambridge, with its splendid, wide-spreading elms and all the rosy brick buildings of Harvard University. Here, in an old wooden house where Washington had stayed when he took command of the American army, lived a young Harvard professor, Henry Wadsworth Longfellow. He was scholarly and gentle, his home was simple and elegant, and he traveled now and then in Europe. Life for him was pleasant and peaceful as was life in Cambridge generally, where rooms were full of books, conversations were of bookish things, and the sharpest sounds to be heard were the musical tinkling of bells as the cows ambled home at twilight, the lullaby of the crickets, or the creaking of sleds in the snow.

Afternoons, after lectures, the young professor rode horseback. Then all his vivid fancies took shape in poetry. He had been born in Portland, Maine, and had never forgotten his old home town with its glimpses of the sea. He was forever thinking of

"Spanish sailors with bearded lips
And the beauty and mystery of the ships
And the magic of the sea."

His house was full of children. Every evening at twilight he heard, in the room above him, the patter of little feet. Then he saw by the lamplight his children on the stairs. A rush and a raid from the doorway, they were climbing over his chair—Alice, laughing Allegra, and Edith with golden hair. The poet had friends in Cambridge, James Russell Lowell and Oliver Wendell Holmes, who were writers like him. And, over in Concord, were Emerson, Hawthorne, and Thoreau. They were a congenial group.

Of all seasons in the year, the poet loved October. When the leaves turned scarlet and yellow and the haze of Indian summer

Standing apart from New England writers of his time, was Edgar Allan Poe with his love of the supernatural as in short stories like *The Goldbug* and his magically interpretive rhythms as in *The Bells.*

lay over all the meadows, he was most deeply stirred. *Hiawatha*, his Indian love story, is a poem of October; a poem of golden harvests, autumn quiet, and smoke of campfires. With gentle sympathy, Longfellow sang of love and sorrow and parting. He did not, like Emerson, strive for any philosophy. He only put into words of wonderful, flowing music the stories of his country, of John Alden and Priscilla, Evangeline, and Hiawatha.

But, with the Civil War, that great New England period of American literature ended. Longfellow, Emerson, and Hawthorne still lived on, but a new note was to be struck in the writing that came later; for, great as these men were, they wrote in the manner of English and European writers. None of them, save Emerson, who had traveled in the West, had had a glimpse of the vast America stretching, over plains and mountains, away to the Pacific. They were of one section only: they all belonged to New England. But, one day, Thoreau remarked, "I have heard an alarm or a trumpet note ringing through the American camp!" Thoreau had met a new poet, a man who lived in Brooklyn, a friend of bus drivers and pilots, who shouted his words to the sea as he raced along the sands. This man was Walt Whitman, born in 1819, on a Long Island farm. No single section, but the whole vast America was in Walt Whitman's heart.

"Great poetry," he cried, "is the result of a national spirit and not the privilege of the select and polished few!" He sang, not of knights and heroes, but of the common man, the working man and working woman. "The commonplace I sing," he said, "the common day and night—the common earth and waters—your farm, your work, trade, occupation, the democratic wisdom underneath, like solid ground for all." His vision was so huge, so tumultuous, he could hardly get it into words, and he wrote, with no care for old forms of rhyme or rhythm, in a kind of poetical prose that was new in the world of letters. His poems in *Leaves of Grass* were full of the mighty thrill of universal life.

They burst forth without the restraint New England poets knew. America's distinctive contribution to the world, he said, would be to carve out from the common man something new and uncommon.

Writers did not know what to make of Whitman. Emerson admired him, but Whittier destroyed his book, and Thoreau both admired and disliked him. "Well, he looks like a MAN!" Abraham Lincoln said.

But, whatever was thought of Whitman, he had, indeed, sounded a trumpet that ended the type of writing for which the New England group was famous. After the Civil War, different parts of the country began all at once to be heard from. Joaquin Miller and Bret Harte wrote of the West; James Lane Allen, of Kentucky; Joel Chandler Harris, of the South; James Whitcomb Riley, of the Middle West; and, greatest of them all, from the banks of the Mississippi, came the voice of a young river pilot, Samuel Clemens, who wrote under the name Mark Twain. *Tom Sawyer* and *Huckleberry Finn* breathed wholly of American life and the outlook and feelings of the ordinary, everyday American.

The way was paved, too, by Whitman's independence in casting old verse forms aside, for the modern American poets, Carl Sandburg, Vachel Lindsay, Amy Lowell, and others who are wholly American in their feeling and manner of expression. Recent years have brought us, in the United States, a great desire for a distinctive expression of our own native genius with a growing interest in our own language and all our own colorful folk tales like the lumberman's *Paul Bunyan*, the cowboy's *Pecos Bill*, and the Yankee sailor's *Old Stormalong*.

But, in the days of Longfellow, life at Cambridge was pleasant and peaceful. It looked out across the Atlantic, always facing Europe and keeping its back well-turned to the vast, almost unknown America which lay to the west of New England. So Longfellow, in his day, sang his songs in peace and quiet, stirred by none of the thrill, the tumult, and vitality of the poets of today.

'Way Down South in Dixie

JOEL CHANDLER HARRIS (*American*, 1848-1908)

A LITTLE, red-haired, freckle-faced midget of a boy dashing down the main street of a sleepy Georgia town behind a team of powerful horses and handling the reins with all the confidence of a six-foot hostler! Joel Chandler Harris, you mischievous little monkey! Whose horses have you borrowed? Come down off that box at once! Your mother is horrified.

It was well for Joel that he did not distress that good mother of his too often, for all her hopes were centered on him. Long years ago the boy's father had deserted the two, and his mother had shouldered with splendid courage the burden of their support. She took in sewing and the two lived in a tiny cottage behind the great house of a friend.

Eatonton was a typical little Southern town of the days before the Civil War. It had a courthouse and a town square, a tavern and several wide streets shaded by rows of fine old trees. On either side of the road, behind the trim boxwood hedges, rose stately colonial houses, the white pillars of their piazzas glinting here and there through the screen of odorous cedars, brightly blossoming myrtles and oleanders around them.

A fun-loving, rough-and-tumble lad on the surface was Joel, playing all sorts of pranks with his friends and rolling in the white mud gullies or munching ginger-cakes with the little negro children. But he was a tender-hearted boy at bottom and never forgot a kindness. See him now behind the old school house, showing a wren's nest to three little girls with such delight in the tiny, fragile thing. And how gentle and kind the little girls are to the lad. A simple thing, but he never forgot it!

One day Joel found these words in a newspaper, "Boy Wanted to Learn the Printer's Trade." Here was his opportunity. He was only fourteen years old but he put away his tops and marbles, packed up his little belongings in an old-fashioned trunk, kissed his mother good-bye and was off. He went to work for Mr. Joseph Addison Turner of Turnwold, a fine old plantation, with cotton-fields white as snow in the season, and a group of negro cabins hid in a grove of oak trees behind the house. Mr. Turner published a paper called *The Countryman*, and the little printing office where the boy worked was a primitive place on the roof of which the squirrels scampered and the bluejays cracked their acorns. Not twenty steps from the office door a partridge had built her nest and was raising a brood of young, while more than once a red fox went loping stealthily by to the woods.

It was hard to say whether Joel enjoyed most the out-of-door life on the plantation, tramping about with a boy just his age who knew every path in the countryside, or browsing in Mr. Turner's fine library, for he dearly loved to read. But when the work and play of the day were ended, and the glow of the light-wood knot could be seen in the negro cabins, Joel and the Turner children would steal away from the house and visit their friends in the slave quarters. Tucked away in the nook of a chimney corner, Joel listened with eager interest while Old Harbert and Uncle George Terrell, their black faces a-gleam in the firelight, told their precious tales of Brer Rabbit and all the other lore of beasts and birds handed down from their African forefathers. And sometimes, while the yellow yam baked in the ashes, or a hoe-cake browned on the shovel, the negroes would croon a camp-meeting hymn, or sing a corn-shucking melody.

So passed months and years at Turnwold. And then the Civil War! Joel Harris, a youth, with all the fire and passionate prejudices of boyhood, sitting up on a fence and watching the victorious Northern troops pass by, ploughing ankle-deep through the mud! The defeat of the South meant the end of *The Countryman* and the ruin of Mr. Turner. Joel had to start life anew. One paper after another gave him employment, and then, at last, he began to write for the *Atlanta Constitution* all those lively negro folk tales impressed so vividly on his mind in the old days at Turnwold —the stories of Uncle Remus. To Joel's immense surprise, Uncle Remus made him famous. And so it happened that the little red-haired boy, now grown a man with a wife and children of his own, could offer his mother a real home, and as his fame grew with the passing years, he brought her increasing happiness and fulfilled all her early dreams.

The Hoosier Poet

JAMES WHITCOMB RILEY (*American*, 1853-1916)

BUDDY RILEY was a sturdy, flaxen-haired little boy with wide-open blue eyes. Greenfield, Indiana, where he lived was a region of cornfields, meadows, woodlands, and orchards, and the people there spoke that racy Hoosier dialect of the pioneer days of the Middle West. Hard work and ragged clothes were Buddy's daily companions and his chief delight was a plunge in the "old swimmin' hole."

When he was twenty-two Buddy was seized with the spirit of adventure. He could not go off on a voyage in search of the Golden Fleece, but he went away in a wagon behind a pair of glossy sorrel horses in the company of a traveling doctor who sold patent medicines, a queer old faker with breezy, long, white whiskers. How delightful it was to bowl over the country. Miles and miles of somber landscape were made bright with merry song, and while the sun shone and all the golden summer lay spread out before him, it was glorious.

It was Buddy's business to write "catchy" songs and to act

in funny little plays to draw a crowd around while the doctor sold his wares. Sometimes he took a soap box and pretended it was a hand organ. Again, he wrapped a companion in buffalo robes, led him about on all fours and with a series of alarming "Woo-ahs" told the story of the *Little Boy Who Went Into the Woods to Shoot a Bear!* But when the first thrill of adventure wore off, the business seemed shabby enough and Riley soon left it to give performances of his own.

His first public appearance was in the little town of Monroeville, Indiana, and his audience was composed chiefly of the "rag-tags" of the neighborhood, a gang of rough fellows. The response to his selections was a sickening jumble of cat-calls and hisses, but he kept a stiff upper lip and finished his program. As he sat down, the village blacksmith, one of the few serious people in his audience, rose and said abruptly, "You fellows have had your fun with this young man and I think you have hurt his feelings. He has done his best to please you and has given us a pretty good show. I move we pass the hat." He dropped in two quarters for luck and passed the hat himself. When it had been the rounds and came back to Riley, it was found to contain beans, pebbles, nails, screws, tobacco quids, buttons, pieces of iron, a doorknob, a wishbone and 58 cents in money!

Thus for two years Riley went about to small towns reciting in schools and churches and generally losing money, happy and astonished if he earned enough to purchase a feast of gingerbread. For these entertainments he wrote his own poems, chiefly in the Hoosier dialect with a warmth of tender sympathy, like *Little Orphant Annie*, till at last the tide turned for him and he met with a huge success. During his later days he gave up wandering and settled down to write in his home in Indiana, one of the few gifted Americans who have created a distinctly native literature.

RHYMES OF CHILDHOOD A CHILD WORLD A HOST OF CHILDREN

The Poet of the Sierras

JOAQUIN (Cincinnatus Heine) MILLER (*American*, 1841-1913)

MOUNTED on a little spotted pony, Cincinnatus Miller rode along the trail toward the mining camp. He had run away from his home in Oregon to seek his fortune mining gold beneath the snowy peak of Mt. Shasta in California.

One night a sailor-man from San Francisco drifted into camp and helped himself to the sluice boxes. The miners caught him in the act, tied him to a tree and told him to dig his grave. The digging proceeded but slowly, so Cincinnatus was called in to help. After they had dug a few feet the sailor-man announced mournfully that his sudden departure from this life would be a hard blow for his wife.

"Have you a wife?" asked the lad with interest.

"Yes, she's in Yrebe," a town a day distant from camp.

"You keep on digging," said Cincinnatus. "I'll tell the men."

The miners heard the story and decided to send for the woman. They told the condemned man that if his tale was true and his wife was brought to camp, his life would be spared on condition that they two should remain and do the cooking for the miners. The sailor-man meekly agreed. He preferred to cook rather than be hanged; and so the woman was brought to camp, a cabin was built for her, and to make sure that she was really the sluice-robber's wife, the miners decided to have them married before their eyes. Opportunity now knocked at the door of young Cincinnatus. There was need of a song for the miners to sing to celebrate the wedding. The only books Cincinnatus knew were Shakespeare and the Bible, but various ringle-jingles kept running in his head. Finally he ground out several yards like the following:

Samson, he was a mighty man,
Oh, a mighty man was he-e,
But he lost his beard and he lost his hair,
Likewise his liber-tee-ee;
For a woman she can
Do more than a man,
Than a King and his whole ar-mee-ee.

The sailor provided the music and the song was yelled at the torchlight wedding by a sturdy chorus of miners.

Now Cincinnatus made no glittering fortune at mining of gold but he managed to earn a living until he was eighteen years old, when he went back home to Oregon to get a little "book learning." Confinement in a schoolroom, however, was more than he could bear, and the next year found him enjoying life by driving the pony express. This was dangerous business enough, for he carried

Uncle Sam's mail, an alluring bait in those days for white or redskin highwaymen. Somewhere about this time, too, Cincinnatus made the acquaintance of a famous Mexican bandit named Joaquin (Walkeen) Murietta. This boy he regarded with pity as a brave and ill-used young fellow who had been driven to desperation by wrongs inflicted in his own country too brutal to be told. His sympathy was aroused, his love of daring and romance, and he cast away his burdensome appellation of Cincinnatus, replacing it forever with the far more picturesque name of Joaquin. Henceforth, when he contributed poems to the Eugene City Review, he always signed them Joaquin.

It was in a little cabin which he had built with his own hands on land given him by the Shasta Chief, Blackfoot, that Joaquin first began serious writing. By and by he had saved enough money to cross the ocean to London. Think of him now, coming from the land of far distances and great sweeps, shut up in narrow London lodgings. Whenever he stopped work he saw in place of the fog and smoke the snow peaks of Oregon looming clear against the sky. Imprisoned as he was, he yearned as never before for America's great plains, where there is "room, room to turn round in, to breathe and be free."

"And to east and to west, to the north and the sun,
Blue skies and brown grasses are welded as one,
And the buffalo come like a cloud on the plain,
Pouring on like the tide of a storm-driven main,
And the lodge of the hunter to friend and to foe
Offers rest; and unquestioned you come and you go."

Presently he caused to be printed with his own hard-earned dollars a thin little volume of poems which fortunately attracted the attention of the famous Rossetti family and their literary friends. They were struck by the breezy freedom of the poet from the west and with their help he brought out a book called *Songs of the Sierras*. Suddenly Miller awakened to find himself famous.

Henceforth, he was feasted and dined and entertained everywhere.

One evening he was invited to a grand reception to meet Lily Langtry, the celebrated actress, who had been reciting his poem *Columbus*. When the time came and the guests stood about all well groomed in their evening clothes, Joaquin appeared, to their astonishment, in a red flannel shirt with blue overalls tucked into tall miner's boots and a high crowned broad-brimmed sombrero. Led by his hostess, he advanced to meet Miss Langtry and lifting his hands to his sombrero, he dexterously showered from it a profusion of beautiful rose leaves. At the same time he exclaimed to the delighted lady: "The tribute of the California miners—California, the land of poetry and romance and flowers—to the Jersey Lily."

So it was England which first recognized Joaquin Miller's genius and he returned to America in the full noontide of his glory, to remain the most unique and picturesque figure in all the field of American letters—tall, broad-shouldered, long-haired and bearded like a pard, always in his big sombrero, his high-top boots and coat to match.

At last he settled down with his wife and daughter in a home called "The Heights," high up in the mountains overlooking San Francisco Bay. When a stranger once asked him where he lived he said: "Three miles east and one mile perpendicular." Indeed, he lived nearer the sun than most men and his normal dwelling place was always one mile perpendicular.

The poet who could picture California, "where the plants are as trees and the trees are as towers," had need of a wide canvas and a generous hand when it came to laying on color. These Joaquin Miller possessed; his poetry breathes of the pine-clad slopes of the Sierras. He was as typically Californian as a giant redwood, and it is due to him, more than any other American, that California literature has impressed itself on the world.

*A Tramp of the Middle West

NICHOLAS VACHEL LINDSAY (*American*, 1879-1931)

AROUND the cliff, with a boom and a bang, rattled a gypsy wagon. On the front seat sat a man and a woman, laughing and showing white teeth, and appearing to think this the gayest morning the sun had ever shone on. The woman was covered with bangles and more bedecked than Carmen. Suddenly, at her suggestion, the horses were pulled up short. Before them appeared a fellow tramp, a tall and sunburned young man in yellow corduroy trousers, sombrero and scarlet tie. At his back he carried a pack which seemed to Mrs. Gypsy to contain some delightful mystery connected with the tramping profession.

"What you sellin', boy?" she asked.

Obligingly the Tramp took down his pack and opened it. First he gave Mrs. Gypsy a pamphlet called the *Gospel of Beauty*, then

**Told chiefly from Lindsay's own book,* ADVENTURES WHILE PREACHING THE GOSPEL OF BEAUTY.

he handed her a booklet named *Rhymes to be Traded for Bread.* Was that what he was selling? Mrs. Gypsy was quite dumbfounded. Strange wares indeed for a tramp! Clucking to the horses, she vanished, smiling, down the road.

Vachel Lindsay had started from his home town, Springfield, Illinois, to walk across Illinois, Missouri and Kansas, up and down Colorado and into New Mexico. He had vowed to take with him neither baggage nor money, but to trade the rhymes he wrote for bread, and so to preach his Gospel of Beauty. Surely, he thought, the common man, the farmer of the Middle West had his secret dreams and visions. Vachel would coax these forth; he would urge a flowering of beauty on lonely prairie farms or in ugly little prairie villages.

Though he was a man and a poet he was still a boy at heart. At any moment he might break out strong and enthusiastic, making the heavens ring with a rousing cry of "Rah for Bryan!" or waking the sleeping echoes by shouting, "Liberty and union, one and inseparable, now and forever-r-r!" When he was back home reciting his poems on a stage he would go through extravagant antics, roaming up and down, shouting, gesticulating. He was nothing if not original. Fancy a poet who could end the reciting of a poem on Daniel in the Lion's Den, as if he were leading a football yell, by insisting that his hearers join in the roar with the lions!

We want Daniel, Daniel, Daniel,
We want Daniel, Daniel, Daniel.
Grrrrrrrrrrrrrrrrrrr,
Grrrrrrrrrrrrrrrrrrrr!

Or imagine the great Lord Tennyson shouting like Vachel Lindsay:

Black cats, gray cats, green cats, mi-au,
Chasing the deacon who stole the cow!

But the very important fact was that Lindsay was not English; he was thoroughly American, a native of the Middle West. New rhythms ran in his soul. Something strong and vivid, vital, crude and different had to get out in his poems. If his verses had football rhythms, both he and his country were young, at an age when that was their natural boisterous outlet for expression. Why should he write in the finished, staid, sedate and time-worn cadences of Old England, a land two thousand years old? A poet must shadow forth the spirit of his native land. So had the English done and so must Lindsay do. He was a Voice from the Middle West. The youth of a very young country was in the things he wrote. But the beauty of prairie and wheat-field, of farms and simple farmers, was in his poems, too. He was most sincerely in earnest; he dreamed of beauty and loved it and where American towns were ugly, drab and colorless, the people bound down by labor and blind to the vision of beauty, he wanted to wake them up, to make them love beauty as he did, so that they might express it by making more beautiful villages, more charming and interesting buildings, a lovelier countryside. As he tramped he handed the country folk such poems as the *Proud Farmer*, *The Illinois Village* and *The Building of Springfield*, or he pasted up on their walls in some conspicuous place where everyone must see it his poster with startling drawings called, *The Village Improvement Parade*.

Now he was off to Kansas because Kansas was to him the ideal American state, a state of tremendous crops, of hardy, simple devout, and supremely natural men, all ruled by the crossroads church. In eastern Kansas he tramped past rich fields with neat little hedges, past picturesque orchards and gardens till he came to the vast stretch of prairie, treeless yet beautifully green, and patterned like a carpet with the shadows of the clouds. On and on he walked over unbroken prairie sod, where half-wild cattle grazed. Then came alfalfa fields with lavender haze of blossoms and music of gorging bees. Later he marched for days with wheat waving all around him as yellow as the sun.

Many a night he slept in the hay-loft of a barn, with the wide loft-door rolled open and the golden moon for his friend. It was Romance itself for him, sleeping in a hay-mow. The alfalfa was soft and fragrant, the wind blew clear and clean and the stars shone through the cottonwoods. Before he knew it, it was morning and the birds in the mulberry trees were singing, "Shivaree, Shivaree, Rachel Jane, Rachel Jane!" After a little walk he bargained for his breakfast at a farm house and was on his way again. Sometimes he hoed corn all morning in order to earn his dinner and as he worked, he talked about his Gospel of Beauty. Then when dinner time came, he entertained the farmer's children by telling them a thrilling tale concerning Grandpa Mouse. Using the ketchup bottle to represent Grandpa Mouse, the salts and peppers for little mice and an old black hat for the owls that came swooping down from the moon to eat unfortunate mice, he acted out the story he told till the children around the table were all quite breathless with interest. The moon was the Queen of the Night-owls and Grandpa Mouse bade the little mice beware of the dread Owl-Queen.

She pours the owls upon us!
They hoot with horrid noise,
And eat the naughty mousie-girls
And wicked mousie-boys.

So climb the moon-vine every night
And to the owl-queen pray!
Leave good green cheese by moonlit trees
For her to take away.

And never squeak, my children,
Nor gnaw the smoke-house door:
The owl-queen then will love us
And send her birds no more!

Sometimes Vachel traveled with section gangs on their hand-cars, but usually he walked, tramping the railroad track or striking out over the prairies as they stretched off flat before him.

"Goin' west harvestin'?" the farmers asked of him.

At first he answered no. He had not intended to harvest. But when he saw how the good folk toiled happy and ungrudging he presently answered yes!

And so he tramped on and on till at last he found himself harvesting at the home of a Mennonite farmer. Fine people and deeply religious were these Pennsylvania Dutchmen, Mennonites by faith, who had come out and settled in Kansas. On Sunday morning Vachel went with them to their meeting. There sat all the women on one side of the aisle. The most pious were down in front wearing little black scoop bonnets, but towards the middle of the church their bonnets gained in color. Here was a cream-colored satin, a soft gray or dull moon-yellow, and when the children trooped in, the little girls were wearing headgear of every hue, yet the same scoop pattern still. Opposite the women sat the men, and not a few of these had piously left off their neckties as a particular sign of their doctrines.

Tillie, the farmer's daughter, like all other Mennonite women, had a pretty way of covering her head with a dainty little lace prayer-cap before Bible lessons were read or grace was said at table, and after supper all the family went about in clean bare feet. They had no profane hour in that family. When not at work, they sang hymns. Their religion was always with them.

Out in the fields Vachel worked beside a Mennonite lad, the sturdy son of the household. Together they followed the reaper and built the sheaves into shocks, so stacked that they could not be shaken by any ordinary Kansas wind. And as they worked the boy sang: "The Day Star Hath Risen," while Vachel, catching the spirit that pervaded all work at the farm, sang every hymn he knew. At noon the Mennonite maid came to the field with their dinner. Then they unhitched the mules, Tillie or one of the men offered a prayer of thanksgiving, and they ate in the shade of the thorn-trees.

When in the afternoon they went back to work in the fields, the sun was a roaring lion. Now the men wrestled with the sheaves as though they had the sun by the beard. It was one long struggle with the heat. But at last, after hours of labor, the sun acknowledged defeat. He shone through the hedge as a blur, as a mist-wrapped golden mountain that some fairy traveler might climb wearing enchanted shoes, no longer an enemy, but a fantasy, a vision and a dream!

Those wide-stretching open spaces where the armies of wheat sheaves were marshalled were magic places for the poet despite their sweat and dust. It was all on so vast a scale. There was nothing small in the whole panorama. Vachel thought of the Bible, of the beautiful Book of Ruth and the Jewish feast of the ingathering and he was happy indeed that he had the strength to bear his part in the harvest of a noble and devout household as well as in the feeding of the world.

O, I have walked in Kansas
Through many a harvest field,
And piled the sheaves of glory there
And down the wild rows reeled!

Yet it was gay in Kansas,
A-fighting that strong sun:
And I and many a fellow-tramp
Defied that wind and won.

And we felt free in Kansas,
From any sort of fear,
For thirty thousand tramps like us
There harvest every year.

Our beds were sweet alfalfa hay
Within the barn-loft wide,
The loft doors opened out upon
The endless wheat-field tide.

I loved to watch the windmills spin
And watch the big moon rise.
I dreamed and dreamed with lids half shut,
The moonlight in my eyes.

DONALD CRANE

When Vachel came home to Springfield after that long tramp, the moonlight was still in his eyes. As he had seen the wheat harvest rich and ripe before him, he dreamed of another harvest, a harvest of art and beauty to be gathered there in Kansas. The children now born in the west should be not only farmers, laborers and workers. They should be poets, artists, actors, musicians, gardeners, architects, classic dancers. They should have the vision of beauty deep within their souls and live for the joy of expressing all that beauty to the world. So dreamed the poet-tramp.

Lindsay's unique individuality and indifference to old verse forms is characteristically modern. It goes back to Walt Whitman and that quiet little spinster, Emily Dickinson, singing her songs as she pleased. When Japan was opened to the West in the 19th Century, acquaintance with Japanese poetry revealed to Americans the beauty of simplicity as opposed to Victorian elaborateness. See Vol. VI, page 196.

The Divine Comedy

DANTE ALIGHIERI (*Italian*, 1265-1321)

THERE was to be a May-time festival in Florence at the home of the noble citizen, Folce Portinari. Dante was only nine years old but he went with his father to the merrymaking. Here among the children was the host's little daughter Beatrice, gay and beautiful in her childish fashion, and in her behavior very gentle and agreeable, so that many thought her almost an angel.

The image of this little maid Dante received into his heart with so much affection that from that time forward as long as he lived it never again departed from him. He saw Beatrice only two or three times in all his life and she married another man, yet Dante venerated her as though she had been a saint and never ceased to love her. She died a very young woman, and it became his greatest desire to make her name immortal by writing of her as no woman had ever been written about before. Not until some time after her death did he marry Gemma Donati.

Now Dante was of the lesser nobility, and after his marriage he became involved in the sorry political quarrels of the day, the strife between the Guelphs, the party of the Pope, and the Ghibellines, the party of the Emperor. So bitter became this struggle that Dante was one day banished from Florence, his house was plundered, and he was condemned to be burned alive if ever he should be caught. Poor Gemma was left alone with a brood of little children, and Dante wandered for twenty years an exile from his home. But Gemma, by her foresight, had hidden many family treasures here and there among friends for safe keeping until the first fury of Dante's enemies should abate, and thus she had saved a copy book in which her husband had written seven cantos of a poem which he called *The Divine Comedy*. This little book he had flung together with other papers into an old chest which he had left behind when he went away into exile. One day a nephew of his, helping Gemma to sort their papers, found this poem and read it. To him it seemed so beautiful that he found means to send it to Dante. The poet had never expected to see his work again, but he cried when he found it thus so unexpectedly in his hands:

"Since it has pleased God that it should not be lost, I will do my best to follow up the work according to my first intention."

Thus in his exile Dante finished the poem which was to be so popular that it helped make the Tuscan language in which it was written the language of all Italy. Dante dreamed that he travelled through Hell under the guidance of Virgil. In a vast conical abyss in the center of the earth, sinning souls were punished according to their sin. With passionate force the poet described the scene. From Hell he ascended the Mountain of Purgatory where sin and suffering were less, and so he came at the top to a forest where a sheet of fire barred his path, but Virgil whispered that Beatrice was just beyond. So the poet leapt through the flames, and there, a vision of celestial purity and sweetness, was Beatrice. She took him by the hand and floated with him from star to star till he came at last to the very presence of God, as he knew by the light and glory that flooded his heart. So in a burst of triumph ends the greatest poem of the Middle Ages.

As Villon's poems spread the Parisian tongue to all France, and Chaucer made English a literary language, so Dante, through the popularity of his poems, made the Tuscan tongue the language of all Italy.

A Spanish Hero

MIGUEL DE CERVANTES (*Spanish,* 1547-1616)

A QUAINT, old market place in a little old town in Spain and a crowd of simple folk gaping about a band of strolling players. There sat young Miguel and watched them, open mouthed with interest. A blanket, hung over two ropes in the open square, formed the sole decoration of this theatre, and the actors went through the performance wearing worn old beards and wigs, and clad in naught more elegant than white sheepskin dresses trimmed with gilt leather. Crude! And yet Miguel drank it all in, and the verses of those comedies fixed themselves in his memory. Sometimes the young fellow took a hand himself at writing verses, but he liked adventure best and longed to be up and doing.

As soon as the opportunity offered, Miguel left Spain and was off to Rome to become a page in the household of an envoy of the Pope. But the life of a page meant little more than bowing and scraping, bowing and scraping. It was slow and uneventful enough. How could a boy like Miguel pass his days in such a manner? He longed for action, bold and vital, and so he resigned his post and enlisted as a soldier in a Spanish regiment in Italy.

At this time Pope Pius V was organizing a Holy League against the Turks, whose barbarous conquests and inroads into Europe were alarming all Christendom. This league consisted of the Papal States, Venice and Spain, and their forces were to be commanded by the famous Don John of Austria, a brilliant general who was half brother to King Philip II of Spain. The fleet of these three powers was the largest that had ever sailed under a Christian flag. It consisted of galleys rowed by criminals under sentence, while the oarsmen of the Turkish fleet were all captive Christians who had been made slaves.

The object of the allies was to recover the island of Cyprus from the Turks and to set these unfortunate Christians free. When they set sail, Miguel was aboard one of the vessels, feeling for the first time beneath his feet the deck of a war galley rising and plunging with the bounding waves of the sea.

In the Gulf of Lepanto the allies fell in with the enemy, and engaged in a furious battle. Miguel was acting only as a common soldier on that great day, but he behaved with conspicuous heroism. Placing himself at the head of a dozen men he took a position exposed to the hottest fire of the enemy. From here he boarded one of the Turkish galleys and engaged in a hand-to-hand conflict with the fierce and barbarous foe. In the course of the battle he received three gunshot wounds, two piercing his breast and one shattering his left hand, which was maimed for the rest of his life, but his conduct won for him the applause of all his comrades. The Christian fleet was victorious. One hundred and seventy Turkish galleys were captured and 15,000 Christian galley slaves set free.

A great storm followed this mighty victory, the sea rose with terrific strength, and Don John sailed away with his wounded men to Messina. Here he left Cervantes to recover his health, graciously bestowing upon him a special grant of money in return for his gallant services, but so eager was Miguel to be at the front again, that as soon as his wounds were healed, he was off to rejoin Don John.

And now the Christians once again engaged the Turkish fleet in battle. This time, however, they met with a sorry defeat. It was evident that the Turkish power was not to be broken by sea; so Cervantes and his comrades sailed off to the African coast and began a long campaign against the strongholds on land. For months the white walls of Tunis defied them, and then, at last, the city was conquered and fell. But, alas, the allies held their hard won prize for only too brief a period.

Soon the Turks came swarming in and drove them out again.

Thus passed four years of struggle, during which Cervantes knew all the hardships of war, the joys of victory and the sorrows of defeat. Having been away from home six years, and finding himself now worn and wounded in his country's service, he at length asked leave to return to his native land. This permission was granted him, and with his brother, Rodrigo, he left Naples on a galley called El Sol, bearing letters from Don John to the mighty King Philip II. In these letters Don John recommended the stalwart soldier as "a man of valor, and of signal services."

But just at the very moment when Miguel and Rodrigo were rejoicing at catching a glimpse of the Spanish coast once again, just as they first saw it glistening in the sunshine and smiling a welcome home, there bore down upon them suddenly a squadron of Turkish pirates under a hideous captain who was the terror of the Mediterranean. There followed a desperate fight, but the pirate galleys were far too strong. Cervantes and a number of Spanish comrades were taken prisoners and carried away to Africa.

The young Spaniards now found themselves placed at the

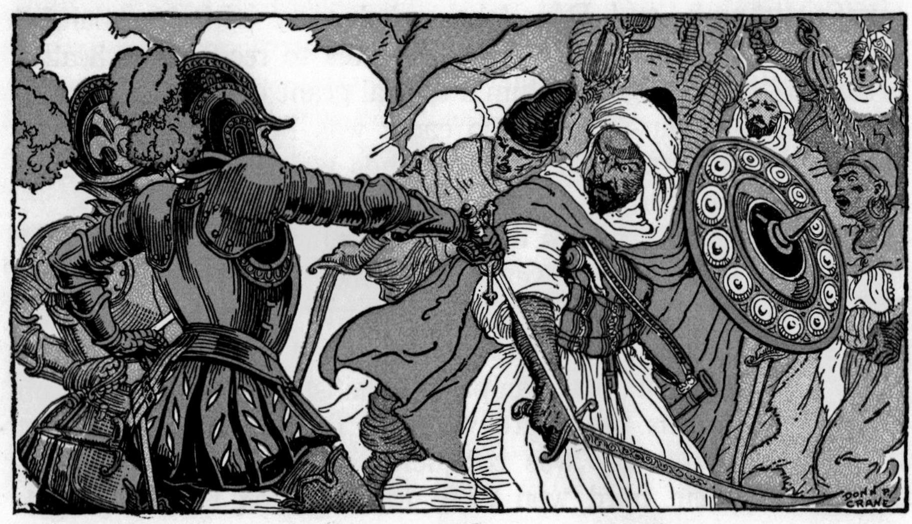

mercy of a savage Greek who was noted for wild ferocity. As the letters from Don John were found on Cervantes' person, he was believed to be a prize of great value, for whom a large ransom might be demanded. Heavily loaded with chains, he was sent off to Algiers, which, for centuries, was the stronghold of the fierce Algerian pirates. Tier above tier, in gleaming white stone, the city climbed up the hillside from the coast, to be crowned by an ancient fortress; and there amid the narrow, dirty streets, the rich, heavily scented Oriental bazaars, Cervantes was held for five long years a prisoner, subject to every caprice of his conqueror, and treated with sternest severity.

During his captivity, however, the sturdy Spaniard never once lost his courage nor his gay and cheerful humor. Adversity brought out the finest qualities of his character. Never was he too miserable to laugh, to smile, or to joke. Persistently, and with great ingenuity, he organized plans of escape, the failure of one plan never deterring him from setting to work at once to prepare another. On one occasion he even succeeded in getting himself and a party of comrades out of the city, but at the critical moment, a Moor who had been engaged to act as their guide, treacherously deserted them. The fugitives were obliged to return to Algiers and Miguel was severely punished.

The next year a sum of money was sent over by the parents of Cervantes, but it was not sufficient to induce the corsairs to release him. Instead, they set his brother, Rodrigo, free. Rodrigo left for home with secret instructions to request that a war vessel be sent from Spain to rescue the other prisoners, and Cervantes himself set about at once making all necessary arrangements to escape when the time should come.

He gathered together about fifty Spanish fugitives and concealed them in a cave outside the city. Here they lived all huddled together for six months while they waited, and Cervantes actually managed to have them supplied with food during all that weary time. At last, after weeks of patient endurance, came the day when the ship was to be expected. Cervantes and his comrades were filled with joy. And then came another blow. Just when freedom seemed so certainly in sight, a traitor betrayed their secret to the pirates, a force of armed Turks discovered their hiding place and captured them one and all. Cervantes immediately took on himself the blame for their scheme of flight. He alone, he declared, was responsible for the plan. The Turks threatened torture, even death, but still he refused to implicate any one of his comrades.

Now the governor of Algiers in those days was a terrible old fellow, one Hassan Pasha, who did not hesitate, as a rule, to hang, impale or mutilate any who were unfortunate enough to be his prisoners. It was to the feet of this monster that Cervantes found himself dragged. But he stood before him holding his head so high, so utterly quiet and calm, that the tyrant was overawed by his astounding fearlessness and did nothing more terrible than utter some hideous threats.

At last, at the end of five years, friends and relatives in Spain raised sufficient ransom money to set the captives free. And thus, after eleven long years' absence, Cervantes made his way home. He reached Spain to find his family impoverished, his patron, Don John of Austria, dead, and no one to speak a good word for him to the haughty and selfish King Philip. Spain at this time, in 1580, was at the very height of her power, dominating the world by land and sea, wringing gold, gold, gold from her people at home and bearing it in great treasure ships from her distant colonies in Mexico and Peru. Imperial ambition and the worship of force were the keynotes to Philip's character, and he had little time to waste thought on a worn-out soldier like Miguel. What heartaches were now in store in Spain for the gallant Spaniard! His services, his work, his sufferings were all forgotten—and yet from these trials also he emerged

sweetened and strengthened, still in possession of his gay courage and his dauntless good humor.

In the most straitened circumstances, he married and settled down, and now there was naught to do, but to take up once more his old pastime of writing. The most popular Spanish writer of the day was one Lope de Vega. He turned out plays by the score and was rich and honored, with many powerful friends, while Cervantes had no friends and no crumb of royal favor. In face of these disadvantages, and struggling against poverty, he wrote his greatest work, *Don Quixote*. No sooner did this book appear in 1605, than behold! it found instant favor with the people. But not so with the literary men! No, indeed! They turned up their noses at it. Quoth Lope de Vega, the Great, from his height of superiority: "No poet is so bad as Cervantes nor so foolish as to praise *Don Quixote*."

The books the good people in those days read, were mostly pompous old romances of chivalry, recording the absurd adventures of wonderful knights-errant who wandered about the world rescuing captive princesses from castles and performing the most impossible deeds of prowess. Cervantes, with his knowledge of life as it really was, found that these tales tickled his humor.

They made him laugh, good naturedly indeed, but still they made him laugh, with their solemnity, their stupidity, their perfect impossibility. It was to show up the absurdity of such books that he wrote Don Quixote, but so fertile was his imagination and so varied had been his own experiences, that at the same time he succeeded in getting into his work a wonderfully graphic picture of Spanish life in his day, bringing in all classes of society, and recounting many of his own adventures as a soldier. Moreover, the broad humanity he had learned in his hard Algerian experiences, permeated with its sweet spirit all of the story.

See him, old Don Quixote, a ridiculous figure in a way and yet a most delightful and great-hearted old gentleman filled with generous and high-minded sentiments. In spite of the absurdity of his adventures he is always courteous and kindly, the champion of the down-trodden and the protector of the weak. From the name Don Quixote the word "quixotic" has crept into nearly every language in the civilized world and conveys precisely the knight's character. It means a man with impossible, extravagantly romantic and chivalrous notions, who is yet a true champion of the right. Great as the book was, however, nobody guessed in those days that it was to be one of the greatest books in the world, translated into more foreign languages than any other, except the *Bible* and *Pilgrim's Progress*.

Cervantes continued to live for some time after this in squalid poverty, cooped up with his family in the poorest part of Vallodolid. In 1616 he died in Madrid and was buried with no ceremony. No stone or inscription marks his grave. Thirty years later, when Lope de Vega died, grandees bore his coffin, bishops officiated at his funeral and the ceremonies lasted nine days. Ah! when will the world learn to judge the real value of men! Today, Lope de Vega with all his splendor, is quite forgotten, while Miguel de Cervantes is honored everywhere.

DON QUIXOTE *retold by Judge Parry, illustrated in color by Walter Crane.*

Faust

*JOHANN WOLFGANG VON GOETHE (*German,* 1749-1832)

ON CHRISTMAS Johann's grandmother gave the children a puppet show. It was set up in the back room adjoining the front hall, where the little old lady lived and where the children delighted to play. A marvelous thing it seemed to the boy and his sister, Cornelia. They could make up their own plays, they could dress the puppets as they chose, they could manage the wires that moved them. Johann even invented new scenery out of pasteboard—pretty summerhouses with pilasters and flights of steps and other decorations. The neighbors' children were sometimes invited in to see the show, but the older ones were so noisy that their din often spoiled the performance and Johann soon barred them out admitting only tiny tots whom nursemaids could keep in order.

Johann lived in an ancient wood and plaster house in Frankfort-on-the-Main. Just beside the front door, and projecting on the street, was a cage, a great square cage of wooden lattice. Cooped up in this, like two little birds, Johann and Cornelia often played. Once when Johann was very small, he threw a whole set of toy pots and mugs one by one out the lattice to hear them go smash on the pavement. From the rear, the house commanded a view over neighboring gardens to the walls of the city and far away over the fertile green plain beyond. On the second story was Johann's favorite retreat, a room where he learned his lessons, watched thunderstorms and sunsets and his neighbors in their gardens, now tending flowers, now rolling skittleballs or playing games of nine-pins.

Frankfort was a fine old town for Johann to roam about in. He loved the great bridge over the Main, the busy market places, the Jewish quarter teeming with alien faces, and the beautiful

**Told chiefly from* DICHTUNG UND WAHRHEIT *(Poetry and Truth) Goethe's Autobiography.*

square of the Römer, its ancient buildings finely carved of wood, some weather stained a rich brown and others painted in vivid colors. On fair days when the city was crowded with people, he liked to creep into the Piper's Court in the Town Hall, whither came deputies from Nürnberg, Worms and Bamberg, with gifts sent to gain for the merchants of those cities the right to sell wares at the fair without the paying of duty. Johann's mother's father was the Schultheiss or Imperial Magistrate and Johann was proud to see him sitting up high on a seat, a step higher than all the judges who occupied the benches running around the room. Suddenly music was heard. There came three pipers in cloaks of blue and gold, one playing a shawm, one a bassoon, and one a bombard or oboe. In their wake, the deputies followed, bearing their gifts, a handsomely turned wooden goblet filled with pepper, some antique silver coins, and a pair of gloves such as the Emperor might have worn.

Later in the day the children never failed to visit their grandfather's house. After Grandma had emptied the pepper into

the spice boxes, they might be given the goblet or one of the ancient coins. As to the gloves worthy of an Emperor, Grandfather wore these in the garden when he grafted roses or trained a peach tree to grow fan-shaped against a trellis.

Such sights as Johann saw gave fire to his fancy and he was great at making up stories. Once, he said, he dressed himself up in his Sunday best breeches, and green coat with brass buttons, his buckled shoes on his feet and his hair all carefully powdered. In such style, he insisted, he ran away in quest of an elfin dancer, who appeared for a moment on his hand and danced about in sprightly fashion from one finger-tip to another before she vanished from sight. He had been led, he said, through a marvelous gate in the town wall and over a bridge of golden spears into a marvelous garden. Here the dancing girl had appeared again and played at toy soldiers with him, till the little Greek warriors came to life and galloped away on horseback, with Achilles and the Queen of the Amazons at their head. This tale he told in so realistic a fashion that more than one of his comrades went off in search of the marvelous gate.

When Johann was ten years old, the King of Prussia, Frederick II, made war on the Emperor of Germany. The French came to the assistance of the Emperor and occupied Frankfort. Then there was great to-do in the town and a certain Frenchman, Count Thorane, was quartered in Johann's house. For several years the French remained in Frankfort and Johann's grandfather, the Schultheiss, gave the boy a free ticket to admit him to the French theatre. Here he learned French and saw the plays of Racine, Molière and other famous French writers. He made acquaintance, too, with a lively French boy whose mother was an actress, and in his company he investigated all the ins and outs of the theatre.

There were always plenty of sights, indeed, to be seen in Frankfort, and a boy like Johann, lively and inquiring of spirit, eagerly investigating everything, wishing to experience all the fullness of life and loving its beauties, missed none of them. In Frankfort the imperial coronations were held, and when Johann was fifteen, he saw the son of Frances I and Maria Theresa crowned as heir to the Empire. He beheld the great procession enter the city—soldiers and officials and lackeys and sixteen six-horse state carriages, the Emperor and his son in a magnificent carved and gilded coach with a whole mirror forming the back, and the top and inside upholstered with crimson velvet. He saw the imperial pair returning from the ceremony at the cathedral, walking under the gold embroidered canopy borne by twelve judges, and he managed even to make his way into the great hall of the Römer and look on at the banquet that followed the ceremony.

But the thing that moved Johann most deeply in his youth was seeing the puppet play of Faust, an old, old German legend. Dr. Faust, so the little wooden puppets told the story, was a professor, foolish and arrogant of mind, searching into all things in heaven and earth, desiring all power and all knowledge. In his madness he turned to magic and one night he conjured up the devil with whom he made a compact. Mephistopheles was to give him all power and every pleasure he might desire for twenty-four years but after that Faust was to belong forever to the devil. Now, with the devil's aid, Faust ascended into the sky in a car drawn by dragons and spent a week among the stars. He visited every part of the earth, flying on the back of a winged horse. He played all sorts of tricks of magic. But at the end of the twenty-four years he had to pay for his pleasures. Mid a terrible hissing and whistling he was carried away by devils, and a great display of fireworks represented the Hell to which he was being borne.

This play stuck in Johann's mind. He could not forget it.

At sixteen he was sent to the University of Leipsig to study law, but he, like Faust, could not content himself with the knowledge of the schools, and so he went through a time of revolt, of mental storm and stress. He felt there was a great secret in the universe which was written in none of his books. Nature, he was sure, had some high secret to tell if one could only get closely in touch with her, some simple message that would render the weary plodding of the schools absurd, put an end to the sorrows of humanity and bring universal joy. With the story of Faust in his heart, he now saw in Faust not a mere seeker after personal power and pleasure, such as the legends presented, but a symbol of himself, his own reasoning, doubting, denying intellect, his own heavenly aspiring soul. Faust was no longer a sinner but a searcher after truth, misunderstood and maligned. When Johann went from Leipsig to Strassburg to pursue his studies, the legend of Faust which had lived for two hundred years in the hearts of the German people, was still his favorite theme. In his early period of mental tension, coupled with high soaring dreams, he began writing down bits of the poem. For more than sixty years it haunted him, no matter what else he wrote. When he went to Weimar to become a councilor of state for his friend, the Duke of Saxe Weimar, and later director of the court theatre there, he took a chaotic manuscript of Faust with him. Through the days of his happy friendship with the poet Schiller when Weimar became the center of the intellectual life of Germany, through the days of his travels in Italy when he knew his own soul calmed down from its early days of revolt, he was writing on Faust, and the changing story reflected the changes in his soul. But not until 1790, when he was forty-one years old, did the Book *Faust, A Fragment*, appear; not until he was fifty-nine did Part I of the drama *Faust* find way to print, and not until he was an old man of eighty-three was he able to read to his daughter the whole of the second part. So the story of Faust embodied all he thought from boyhood to old age and the completed drama is the greatest thing in German literature, scaling, as it does all the heights and depths of a man's soul in its search to know itself.

The Story of Faust

IN a high-arched Gothic chamber where the sunlight came but dimly through painted windows, lived Herr Professor Doktor Faust, hemmed in by mouldy books, worm-eaten, dusty, old. He had studied philosophy, law and medicine with every other rigamarole of human knowledge and yet could only cry:

*"*Here I stand with all my lore,*
Poor fool, no wiser than before."

Human existence seemed to chain him to the earth. He

**Poems in this story are from the translation by Anna Swanwick.*

wished to know the secret that would free him from galling fetters of the flesh. He would fly through the air in a chariot of fire. He would glide with the moonlight over the meadows. He would pierce through the outward appearance of things to everlasting truth. He would be one with a life unlimited and divine. All these secrets he found written down in none of his university's musty tomes.

"I, the image of God," he cried, "who thought myself almost the mirror of eternal truth, would delight myself in heavenly light and purity, stripped of mortality!"

Dissatisfied and striving ceaselessly, he turned to magic and conjured up the Earth-spirit; but so giant-like and vast a vision only made the man feel shrunk and dwarfed before it. In despair he thought to kill himself, but as he put the poison to his lips, his hand was stayed. He heard the happy bells that usher in the Easter morn, with youths and maidens singing:

"Christ is arisen,
Blessèd the loving one."

Such heavenly songs recalled the simple faith in God that had been his in childhood. Tears filled his eyes; he put the goblet from him. He would remain on earth.

Now, Doctor Faust had as his servitor, a youth named Wagner, a narrow-minded bookworm, satisfied with mouldy knowledge. On the afternoon of Easter Wagner went to walk with Faust outside the city gates. Old Winter's cold was disappearing and the budding joy of Spring lay over all the valley. There were no flowers as yet to give a color to the meadows, but the motley throng in gala dress invested all with brilliant hues. From out the gate they streamed in bright array,—soldiers, students, beggars, burghers.

"Look," cried Faust in loving sympathy. "Look how the throng on nimble feet spreads over field and garden. How the boats glide gaily on the river, and even there from yonder far-off hill come flashing back the brilliant hues of colored garments."

Underneath the linden tree were peasant lads and lassies dancing.

The shepherd for the dance was dressed
With ribbon, wreath, and colored vest,
A gallant show displaying,
And round about the linden-tree
They footed it right merrily,
Juch-he! Juch-he!
Juch-heisa! Heisa! He!
So fiddle bow was braying.

Swift in the circle they advanced,
They danced to right, to left they danced,
And all the skirts were swinging,
And they grew red and they grew warm,
Panting, they rested arm in arm,
Juch-he! Juch-he!
Juch-heisa! Heisa! He!
To hip their elbow bringing.

At length the air grew chill and evening mists began to steal like ghostly wraiths across the valley. Then Faust espied a strange black poodle slipping in and out amid the grain and circling ever nearer. A fateful beast he seemed, a creature drawing magic snares to make a band around their feet. Say, was not that a track of fire he left behind him on his path? Nay, Wagner could see nothing save a simple dog who wagged his tail.

"Come hither, sir!" cried Faust. The poodle came and followed him back home.

And now the tumult in the heart of Faust was calmed.

"In evening quiet, all unholy thoughts must die," he cried. "The love of man doth sway us and love to God inspires the soul."

But at his words the dog began to scamper noisily and sniff about.

"Peace, poodle, peace," cried Faust. "Go lay thee down behind the stove."

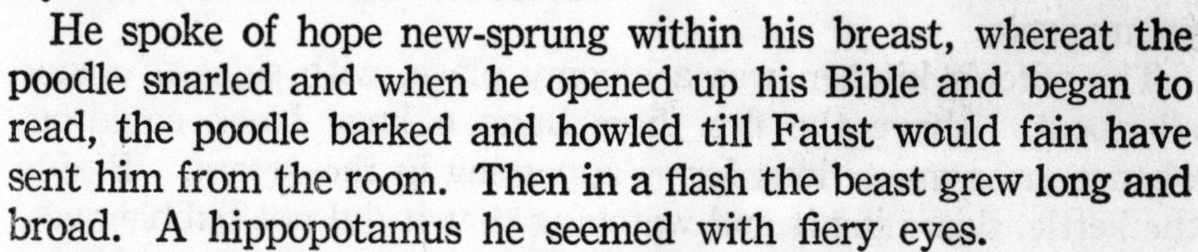

He spoke of hope new-sprung within his breast, whereat the poodle snarled and when he opened up his Bible and began to read, the poodle barked and howled till Faust would fain have sent him from the room. Then in a flash the beast grew long and broad. A hippopotamus he seemed with fiery eyes.

"What devil have I brought home?" cried Faust.

A devil indeed. The creature swelled and swelled until he faded into mist, and when the mist had sunk, there stepped from out the shadow of the stove one, Mephistopheles, the Lord of all Destruction, Prince of Darkness, Master of Deceits and Adversary of God. To him all yearning towards a high ideal in men was but a laughing stock. Hi, yi! The strivings of these little human grasshoppers who fain would fly but could not, seemed antics quite ridiculous. Said he to Faust:

"Come, stop your brooding. Go out and see the world. Eat, drink, be merry. Let pleasure cure your sorrows."

He would make the man eat dust! He would stop his strivings after truth and freedom with mere animal delights, enjoyment of the senses. Faust was desperate. He did not really believe the devil's lure could bring him peace and yet he could not go on

Three great operas tell the story of Faust in music—*Faust*, by Gounod; *Mefistole*, by Boito; and *The Damnation of Faust*, by Berlioz. Christopher Marlowe, in Shakespeare's time, wrote a play, *Dr. Faustus*.

living as he had. And so he signed a solemn compact with his blood. The devil should serve him faithfully so long as he should live on earth, but when his earthly life was ended, Faust would yield himself to Mephistopheles forever, on this one condition only—the devil should sometime bring to him such happiness that he would stretch himself upon a bed of ease completely satisfied, and wish the passing moment to endure forever.

The compact made, off sallied Mephistopheles with Faust to taste the revelry of Auerbach's Cellar in Leipsig, where the students of the university caroused. But here amid the maudlin crowd, the drinking and the singing, Faust was only bored.

"The man's too old," the devil said, and so he took him off to seek from some old witch a magic potion that should make him young again.

The witch's kitchen was a gloomy place, with signs of magic all about. Above the fire there hung a huge black cauldron, whence arose mysterious forms appearing in the steam. Beside the kettle, skimming it and watching that it did not bubble over, sat an ape, while other apes crouched near.

"It seems your dame is not at home," said Mephistopheles.

The apes made answer: "She's gone to carouse out of the house, through the chimney and away."

But soon they fell to playing and quite forgot the cauldron.

All at once it overflowed. A flame shot up the chimney. With horrid cries the witch came down, crying through the fire:

"Ough, Ough, Ough, Ough,
Accursèd brute! Accursèd sow!
The cauldron dost neglect? For shame,
Accursèd brute, to scorch the dame!"

Then seeing Faust and Mephistopheles, she shrieked:

"Whom have we here? Who's sneaking here? Whence are ye come? With what desire? The plague of fire your bones consume!"

And in the boiling pot she dipped the ladle, throwing flames about. The monkeys whimpered fearfully, but Mephistopheles began to rage and smash the pans and glasses.

"Skeleton! Vile Scarecrow! Dost not know thy master?"

As he spoke, she recognized him for the devil, and crying in a master's voice, he bade her brew a magic potion for his friend. With gestures wild and weird, she drew a ring upon the ground and summoned Faust to come inside. Then, calling to the apes, she placed a book upon the back of one and read a charm from out its pages, while the others held the torches. As she read, the glasses rang, the cauldron sang, and Faust received a magic liquid from which rose a little flame the moment that he put it to his lips.

Now young again, he walked the streets with all the swagger of a youth, and soon he met a pretty lass, sweet Gretchen, soft of cheek and red of lip. He loved her in a moment and must have her for his own. 'Twas Gretchen in the garden, Gretchen at her spinning wheel, Gretchen at a neighbor's house. They loved each other dearly. Ah, but Mephistopheles knew well that warm and tender love must ever be an enemy to the devil. He feared lest real unselfish love within the breast of Faust should save the man and wrest him from his power. And so he planned to carry him away and fill his mind with foolish pleasures till he quite forgot the girl. But this he did not do, alas! till he had wrought sore havoc for pretty little Gretchen—slain her brother in a quarrel, tempted her to give a sleeping potion to her mother by means of which the woman died, and so left Gretchen in misery and alone.

Weeks passed for Faust in foolish pleasures. Gretchen he forgot. Then came the last of April and Walpurga's Night, the Witches' Fête, when all the witches gather on the Brocken, a rocky barren mountain peak. To that mad spot came Faust and Mephistopheles, as jaunty travellers abroad to see the sights.

The night was dark. A sad young moon gave only troubled light. With every step the wanderers ran sharp against a rock

or tree. But soon they saw before them, gleaming eerily, now here, now there, upon the path, a dancing fire, a goblin Wisp. The devil called the little fellow, bidding him to light them on their way.

Trees on trees flew by and cliffs on cliffs. The rocks long-snouted, row on row, how they snorted and how they blew! The hill was magic mad. Tu-whit, Tu-whoo,—the owls! From bushes, salamanders peered like eyes of fire, the roots of trees seemed writhing snakes to coil and seize. Through moss and heath ran swarms of many-colored mice; fireflies, like wild things, danced above; the goblin Wisps increased and puffed their pale unearthly flames; rocks and trees made faces, and all things whirled and flew.

"Grasp tight my doublet," cried Mephistopheles to Faust. "At last we've reached the central peak."

Through all the chasms gleamed a strange and lurid light, pervading with its beams the gorges of the gulf below. Here vapors rose, there clouds went floating by. Now, like a fountain, light burst forth on high and scattered down a shower of golden sparks. Then all around the rocky walls blazed forth.

"Doth not the devil light his palace grandly for his fête?" cried Mephistopheles. "Thou'rt lucky to have seen the sight. Cling to those rocks, my friend, lest you be hurled down into some abyss. The murky vapors thicken. The storm blasts howl and roar. The owlets fly in wild affright. Trees are splintered, roots upriven. One crashing ruin overwhelms them all. Hark, along the mountrain streams a raving magic song."

Now to the Brocken the witches hie,
The stubble is yellow, the corn is green;
Thither the gathering legions fly,
And sitting aloft is Sir U′-ri-an seen;
O'er stick and o'er stone they go whirling along,
Witches and he-goats, a motley throng.
Alone old Baubo's coming now;
She rides upon a farrow sow,
A goodly sow and mother thereon,
The whole witch chorus follows anon.

The way is broad, the way is long.
What mad pursuit, what tumult wide!
The wind is hushed, the stars grow pale,
The pensive moon her light doth veil,
And whirling on, the magic choir
Sputter forth sparks of drizzling fire.

"Stay, stay," called a voice from below. "Pray, take me with you. Three centuries I've tried in vain to climb this height. I hobble after many a day. Already the others are far away!"

But the witches replied:

"Broom and pitchfork, goat and prong,
Mounted on these we whirl along.
Who vainly strives to climb tonight
Is evermore a luckless wight."

Rounding the topmost peak, they appeared and let themselves down to earth, to cover all the heath with their mad swarm of witchery.

They crowd and jostle, whirl and flutter; they whisper, babble, twirl and splutter; they glimmer, sparkle, stink and flare, a true witch-element! Beware!

"Stick close," cried Mephistopheles, "or we'll be parted."

A hideous din of instruments snarling rent the air. In a circle round about, a hundred fires arose, with dancing, chattering, cooking, drinking round the glimmering coals. From fire to fire the devil led his friend in search of entertainment, till at last they spied a witch who wore a look of beauty and of youth. With this alluring dame Faust fell to dancing madly till there crawled a red mouse from her lips. Then, bah! he found her loathsome and danced with her no more. And as he went away alone, he seemed to see a maiden sad, forlorn, apart from all the crowd. Who was it? Was it Gretchen? He thought of her again, his Gretchen. Vainly now the devil told him that the form he saw was but a phantom, for the heart of Faust had wakened up to memory and was filled with thoughts of Gretchen only. What had become of her? In some strange way he knew. Mother and brother dead, deserted by her lover, she had wandered here and there forlorn, so sunk in misery that she had grown half-crazed and lay now on a bed of straw, like any common criminal in prison.

"Hound! Monster!" cried Faust to Mephistopheles, beside himself with grief. "You left her thus to die without my help and lulled me all the while with tasteless dissipations. Take me to her and save her or woe be unto you."

On magic coal-black steeds they mounted to the air and rushed along. The devil put the jailor at the prison to sleep, Faust took the keys and entered in to Gretchen. How she was changed, that pretty little Gretchen. Her thoughts ran here and there, a crazy round. She scarcely knew her lover, nor would she follow him although the door was open wide and freedom just beyond. She had committed sins for him. She had deceived her mother and committed sin on sin. Until the morning dawned Faust lingered choked with grief to see the ruin he had wrought and urging her to flee. She would not go. And then came Mephistopheles in search of Faust. At sight of him whom all her soul abhorred, poor Gretchen called on God: "Father, I'm thine! Deliver me!"

There came a host of angels to set the soul of Gretchen free, but, as before, the devil flew away with Faust.

*On a flowery meadow high up in the Alps, the weary Faust sought sleep, his heart sore rent with keen remorse and rankling horror. The holy stars shone clearly in the sky, the moon reigned in full majesty, and moon and stars were mirrored in the lake below. Then came a group of tiny graceful forms to flit on airy wing around the sleeper's head and calm the tumult of his pain. Fairies of sleep they were and Ariel sang a magic lullaby.

When in vernal showers descending
Blossoms gently veil the earth,
When the field's green wealth uptending
Gleams on all of mortal birth;
Tiny elves where help availeth,
Large of heart there fly apace;
Pity they whom grief assaileth,
Be he holy, be he base.
Now the hours are cancelled; sorrow,
Happiness have passed away,
Whole thou shalt be on the morrow,
Feel it! Trust the new-born day!
Gird thee for the high endeavor,
Shun the crowd's ignoble ease!
Fails the noble spirit never,
Wise to think and prompt to seize.

*Part II begins here.

As he sang, the east was dyed with splendor that proclaimed the rising of the sun. Thereat the elves took flight and crept away to hide in blossoms for the day.

Faust awoke. Before him lay the world in glimmering dawn. The woods resounded with a thousand voices. Mist wreaths shrouded all the valley; earth showed itself enameled with unnumbered dyes; on flower and leaflet hung the dewdrop pearls. And now the snowy mountain peaks caught the clear radiance of the new-born day. In blinding rays it blazed, and where the cataract went roaring down from fall to fall with showers of cooling spray, there glanced the rainbow's many-colored arch. With solemn joy, Faust drank in all the glories of that sight. A high resolve awoke within his heart. He would press on to being's very height.

But Mephistopheles had other lures in store. He had not satisfied the man with pleasures in the little world of common men. Then he would take him to the great world of the Emperor's court.

It was Shrove Tuesday when the two arrived at court, a gala day with preparations for a masquerade afoot. The palace was bedecked to represent a rustic scene at noon. Thither came a host of jolly Punchinellos, fishermen, woodcutters, gardeners and ladies dressed as flower girls from Florence with baskets full of blossoms on their heads. And after these there came an elephant with Prudence on her neck as driver and Victory on her back, a woman radiant with broad white wings. On either side of her walked Hope and Fear in chains. But these had scarce appeared when Mephistopheles began his tricks. He conjured up a hideous dwarf with two great heads. The monster pressed up close to Lady Victory and mocked at her so that the herald whose duty was to keep the peace, struck at the fellow with his staff. Thereat one head became a crawling snake which wriggled off in dust, the other showed itself a bat and flew away. Great consternation seized the crowd at such a sight but wonders did not cease. Above

their heads appeared a magic chariot drawn by four great dragons; beside the charioteer rode Faust as Pluto, god of Wealth, and Mephistopheles, a living skeleton, upon a box of treasure.

The charioteer began to snap his fingers and there came a glance and glitter all about the car. Bright jewels appeared to fall on every side—gold spangles, earrings, necklaces and crowns. The crowd pressed forward eagerly to grasp the treasure. Ah, but look!—what one clutched frantically took wings and flew away, a worthless butterfly. A chain of pearls dissolved and turned to crawling beetles in a courtier's hand, and as the foolish fellow cast them from him lo, they buzzed and hummed about his head!

Amid such tricks as these, the chariot came to earth. Then Faust alighted while the dragons lifted down the chest.

And now, with song and music, came the vanguard of the Emperor,—young fauns with broad and merry faces, pointed ears, snub noses and oak leaves on their heads; satyrs having feet like goats and hairy legs, all dancing two and two; a crowd of little gnomes with miner's lamps and mossy garments, tripping helter skelter; after them a bodyguard of wildmen, giants from the mountains with leafy aprons and pine tree trunks for clubs. Lastly, came the Emperor himself, a careless, pleasure-loving youth, as Pan, the monarch of the woods.

No sooner had the gnomes begun to pry about than they espied a glowing vein of gold that flowed from out the devil's magic chest; and off they ran to fetch the Emperor and show the stream to him. He needed gold, the Emperor, for matters in his kingdom were all topsy-turvy through mismanagement, his people grumbled and the wisemen said that naught but gold could straighten out affairs. And so he went full willingly to see the magic stream.

And now the gold became a shining fountain, seething forth from the abyss and scattering showers of pearls like foam, to sink again and leave a cavern darkly yawning. The Emperor leaned down to see the source whence this rich stream had come. Alas, his beard fell in and bursting into flames flew back again to set his garments all on fire. His people rushed to help him, but the flames appeared on all, a burst of fire that spared no corner of the hall. Loud cries of woe arose, then all at once a magic mist appeared and quenched the flames.

Such wizardry! The Emperor delighted in it all. Next day he

gave the devil and his friend a place at court. Aye, let them stay and entertain the crowd. Since power like this was theirs, pray let them, for amusement, conjure up that loveliest of women, from the ancient land of Greece, fair Helena of Troy. In answer to the Emperor's command, it came about that Faust and Mephistopheles made bold to summon from a magic tripod's smoke, the shades of Helena and Paris, cloud-like forms that moved in rhythmic grace with strains of heavenly music. So lovely was this Helena that Faust quite lost his head for love of her, forgetting that she was a phantom only. Stretching forth his hand he sought to seize her, whereupon there came a loud explosion, both the phantoms vanished into air and Faust fell senseless to the earth.

Now Mephistopheles pretended not to know what ailed his friend and so he bore him, lifeless as he seemed, back to that old building where his one-time servitor, Herr Dr. Wagner labored still. The devil found the doctor with a great experiment in progress. Wagner had been trying to produce a human being by a mixture of the different chemicals, and now he felt success was just ahead. A moment more and he would have his man. The devil slyly added to his work a touch of magic, and in Wagner's bottle, lo, a manikin appeared, the small, transparent figure of a man, all luminous and glowing. Doctor Wagner was beside himself with joy. Behold what he had done!

At once Ho-mun′-cu-lus began to speak. He wished to break his glass like any chick prepared to break its shell and so commence

existence on the earth, but as he looked about he did not like the ugly spot where now he found himself. Herr Wagner's laboratory, ah, indeed, was that, a place where one would wish to live? Nay, rather, he would say farewell to Dr. Wagner. He would stay there in his little house of glass and travel all about the world, nor break his shell until he found the spot of greatest promise where he might with joy begin to live.

Homunculus was small but he was wise. He told the devil what was troubling Faust and how he might be cured. The man would not regain his senses till they took him to the classic land of Greece where he might hope to find his Helena again. A Greek Walpurga's Night would soon be held, he said, a gathering of classic ghosts in Thessaly on dread Pharsalia's Plain where Caesar fought with Pompey. To this spot Homunculus proposed that they should journey. Now the devil was not loth to make acquaintance with these classic witches and compare them with the northern hags of whom he was the master. So the two left Dr. Wagner and set out, the manikin within his shining little house of glass, flying through the air and gleaming like a meteor, the devil bearing Faust inside a magic mantle.

Pharsalia's Plain lay covered with a swarm of ghostly tents, as though the two great Roman armies bivouacked on the field.

Pale bluish watch-fires gleamed about, and everywhere the soil sent up a phosphorescent flame like blood. Here gathered every sort of classic ghost and monster, sibyls and Thessalian witches, sphinxes, griffins, centaurs.

No sooner had the devil laid his friend on classic ground and gone to entertain himself, than Faust regained his senses once again, all eagerness to seek for Helena. He wasted not a moment but set out at once to question where she might be found, and soon he met an aged sibyl who agreed to lead him down the path of shadows to the underworld where dwelt the shades of those who lived no more on earth.

Homunculus, meanwhile, his duty done in bringing Faust and Mephistopheles to classic ground, had started out to seek his fortunes by himself. Still in his house of glass he flew from place to place with but a single thought,—to find the proper spot for him to crack his shell and enter into mortal life. He met with more than one kind sir who offered him advice. A certain wiseman sought with weighty words to win him for a glorious career on land. "Ah, things on land change suddenly!" said he. "There growth is quick and violent and one may find himself a hero overnight!" Even as he spoke, the giant Earthquake, he who dwells within the center of the earth, pushed up his head to see the light of day; and as he hove his mighty shoulders through the ground, he cast a new volcanic mountain up. Hereon there dwelt a race of little Pgymies, over whom the wiseman wished to make Homunculus the King. Alack, no sooner did these Pygmies see

the light of day, than what must they begin to do? Prepare for war. Prepare to fight the Herons, raise the cry that they must take by force the Herons' lovely feathers, to adorn the Pygmy helmets. Pygmy elders held a council of debate and ordered weapons forged. Their little Generalissimo went bustling busily about. The war began and into it the Pygmies dragged the peaceful race of Ants and Dactyls, tiny metal workers no bigger than your thumb. It was a bloody fray, but soon the Cranes of Ibycus, the kinsmen of the Herons, flying high in air, beheld this wanton, unprovoked assault upon their friends. A cloud of Cranes descended to the earth to punish the offenders. Beak and claw they fought. Then, pray, of what avail were Pygmy shields and spears? The little men were put to flight, their army went to pieces, Ants and Dactyls ran away to hide, and in a moment more, a meteor descending from the sky, upturned the mountain, overwhelming all. Lo, where was now the little race that strove by violence? It was no more at all.

Homunculus was breathless with the haste. "With small men, one grows small," he said. "I will have none of such a world of sudden violent upheavals," and he turned away and sought the sea with all its beauties, its slow and ordered processes of peaceful growth and change. Before him stretched the blue Aegean, smiling, glistening in the sun. About, on all the cliffs, the sirens lay at ease, with Nereids and Tritons sporting in the waves. Homunculus was overjoyed with such a sight, so peaceful and so calm. And then arose from out the sea that nymph most lovely of them all, the Queen of Love and Beauty, Galatea, gliding over rippling waters in a chariot of tortoise shell with dolphins for her steeds. So beautiful was Galatea and so grateful was the sheer serenity of all that calm and peace, that here Homunculus was fired with one great overwhelming wish to live. His little house began to glow and grow with deep intensity of longing. In an ecstasy he dashed his shell against the car of Galatea till it broke, his flame

Man's struggle to know himself and the capacities of his own mind and soul, his longing to know the meaning of life, is expressed in the old Faust legend which parallels Goethe's own inner strife and yearnings.

suffused the water and he swam about beginning life with joy where he might have the chance to grow through peaceful change, unto the stature of a man.

Now while all this was going forward, Faust was coming back from Hades with his Helena, a lovely shade. The devil conjured up a mediaeval castle and, amid a shadowy train of Trojan maidens, Faust and Helena disported them and lived a short love idyll. All the beauty of old Greece, its joys of poetry and art, came back to life for Faust in person of his Helena, yet even here, his warmly pulsing northern heart could find no lasting satisfaction. Helena, alas, was but a shade and not a living woman. They had a son, a buoyant bounding little fellow named Euphorion, the very spirit that is Poetry itself, as handsome as Apollo, and forever singing to his little golden lyre. One day in reckless vehemence he climbed a rocky height,—higher still and higher. Presently he saw afar a battle. Martial frenzy seized him. In his longing he would fly to reach the scene of glory. Thus he cast himself upon the air and crashing fell before his mother's eyes. The spell that held fair Helena to earth was broken then. She followed her beloved son back to the underworld and in the fond embrace of Faust was nothing left except her dress and veil.

Thus Faust must know a deep, heart-breaking sorrow once again; but Helena did not depart without bequeathing unto him the old Greek spirit of heroic enterprise. The thing for him was action. Ah, he saw it now. He would go back to Germany and build great dikes, reclaiming from the sea a huge low-lying tract of swamp land that he knew. To get a title to this land was easy, for the Emperor, through issuance of worthless paper money had involved himself in war, from which the devil's magic saved him, and in gratitude he gave the swamp to Faust.

And now the clouded thoughts of Faust grew clear. To do and plan, to drain the swamp and make a home for happy burghers, thousands of them who should dwell forever free and peaceful in

As Goethe struggled to understand life, so did his friend, Beethoven. Bach wrote great religious music with serene acceptance of the world as it is; but Beethoven, afflicted with deafness, challenged and found faith through seeking.

the state that he would found, their happiness secure in industry and not in idleness. It was a glorious vision and it thrilled him through and through. Never had he sought before to use his mighty powers of mind in action for the good of others. Here was joy he had not dreamed of. Seeking pleasure for himself had brought no satisfaction, neither in the small world nor the Emperor's court, nor through the tricks of magic. Even all the arts and poetry of ancient Greece were lovely phantoms that could never satisfy the deepest longings of the heart. But he whose days are all activity with real purpose for the good of men finds life to be no riddle. He has never need to stretch and strain to reach the stars. Each day the knowledge that he needs he finds within his reach and so he journeys toward his final goal, the height of perfect being, slow perhaps and like Homunculus, by gradual and ordered steps, but conscious of his unity with all that lives and never more bound down by any sense of limitation in his human lot. In dreams of what he meant to do for all those happy burghers, Faust cried out with joy:

"Could this be realized, then I might say, 'This moment is so fair, I would that it might last forever'."

Even as he spoke he fell prone to the ground. His earthly life was over. Then the devil said, "His soul is mine. In this last moment he was satisfied." Therewith, he summoned hosts of devils bidding them to bear the soul to Hell. But ah, the joy that Faust had felt at thought of bringing happiness to others was not of the devil's giving. It was not to Mephistopheles that he belonged, and so there came to rescue him a choir of angels singing songs and ever scattering roses. Up and up they bore him from the devil's very grasp, and to the Holy Mountain.

There, amid a throng of sacred forms, appeared sweet Gretchen, purified of all her sins, embodiment of holy and redeeming love, to lead him ever upward where he, too, should cleanse himself of false desires and find the light of everlasting joy, at one with God.

Fjords and Mountain Peaks

BJÖRNSTJERNE BJÖRNSON (Byurnson) (*Norwegian*, 1832-1910)

THE minister's little lad was a dull scholar. One must have the patience of Job to get anything into his head. His teachers were in despair and sometimes his parents thought they must send him to sea to be tamed by the stern discipline of a sailor.

But ah, it was a beautiful spot where he lived in the Romsdal, one of the finest valleys of western Norway, and the boy soaked in all the weird loveliness of the place. There the dark hues of mountain masses crowned with ice and snow, are mingled with the variegated splendor of the green and flower-clad valley. Dark fjords stretch their long arms into the land. From the very edge of their waters the mountains often rise, abrupt and rugged and sombre, with waterfalls and cascades, like silver ribbands, like bridal veils, like sheets of mist, leaping down from the snows and coquetting with the rainbows.

Trolls could live in such a spot and giants of ice and mist. Aye, they could play ball with boulders or snowball with an avalanche. In all the old Norse sagas, eddas and tales the boy felt the thunder of Norway's rivers, the roar of her waterfalls, the sighing of her groves, the shadowy melancholy of her fjords and sombre mountains, and the sunny joy of all her flower-clad valleys.

He was twelve when he went to the grammar school at Molde, a small coast town in Romsdal. Would he ever learn his lessons? Say, would he ever fit himself for the university? His teachers urged but he only said: "They want me to study and read so much, while I would rather write."

Sometimes people flung at the lad the title of Agitator. When he was only fifteen, he organized a club of boys to talk over political matters. Even to those remote valleys of Norway, the revolutions that threatened thrones all over Europe in the year 1848 had sent their thundering echoes and awakened a response. Young Björnson, in a land with a King, was the outspoken leader of the boys who favored a republic and he started among them a paper called *Liberty*, which had to be written painstakingly by hand.

At length, with great difficulty, the Agitator passed the entrance examinations for the University of Christiania. But now he found a new line of activity which awakened all his interest. Since 1814, when Norway had separated from Denmark to become an independent kingdom, she had been struggling to create a national literature, untinged by the color of any foreign influence. Asbjörnson and Moe had already made their pilgrimages among the picturesque villages and quaint little hamlets of Norway, collecting from the peasants the fine old fairy tales of the people, and these had had their effect upon the writings of the day. Yet, save for her ancient stories, Norway had still little literature that was really her own. One might easily trace the finger of Denmark or France or Germany in everything that was done. At this miserable state of things young Björnson's patriotism took flame. Fjords and mountains and peasant-folk! Let Norway have her own literature.

Henceforth the boy whom teachers could not drive to work that did not interest him, labored and worked without ceasing. His first story was *Synnove Solbakken.* It was different from anything else that had ever been done in Norway. Heretofore it had been the fashion for Norwegian authors to write romantic tales of Italy or some other far-off land, but Björnson had the courage to seek his subject right at home. He wrote about Norway and homely Norse peasant life, and how simply, how freshly, with what infinite sympathy for his people! His work at once became popular.

Tall, erect, broad-shouldered son of the frozen North, he could speak with a silver tongue, he could write like no other Norwegian. Three times he edited a paper, once he was director of the National Theatre at Bergen and again of the Royal Theatre at Christiania. Now he began to publish in rapid succession a series of national dramas, the subjects of which were taken from Old Norse or Icelandic sagas. As in his novels, he aimed to depict the modern Norse peasant, so in his dramas he strove to present what was most thoroughly Norse out of Norway's historic past.

As time went on a still more serious purpose took root in his heart. It was no longer his ambition only to please and amuse. He began to see clearly the faults in Norwegian society and to wish to bring home to the people a real desire for reform. So now he spoke out plainly and depicted these faults in his dramas. When he saw the dishonesty of the press, he put all that he saw on the stage in the shape of a play called *The Editor;* when he saw the corruption in the world of trade and commerce he wrote *The Bankrupt*, and, in his drama *The King*, he gave free expression to his ideas about a republic as the ideal form of government.

During the later years of his life Björnson was awarded the Nobel prize for literature and he proved to be one of the greatest poets, dramatists and novelists that Norway ever produced, the

most Norwegian of Norwegians. When he wrote a national song it was sung by the whole nation from Lindesnes to the North Cape and the Land of the Midnight Sun.

A Boy in Russia

LEO N. TOLSTOY (*Russian*, 1828–1910)

LEO TOLSTOY lived with his three brothers at Yasnaya Polyana, the beautiful country estate of his father, Count Nicolay Tolstoy. They were a merry crew of youngsters, always up to something interesting. One day, when Leo was five; Dimitri, six; and Sergey, seven; Nicolay said to his brothers: "I know a secret which will make all men happy when it is discovered. There will be no more diseases and no more troubles. No one will be angry with anyone else, all will love each other, and all will become Ant-brothers."

Doubtless Nicolay meant Moravian-brothers, for he had read of the Moravian brotherhood and their ideals of peace and brotherly love; but, in Russian, the word for Moravia is the same as the word for ant, so they became to Nicolay the Ant-brothers. Nicolay said he had written the great secret of happiness on a green stick, which he had buried by the road on the edge of a certain ravine. He then organized a game called Ant-brothers wherein all the children lay down under a chair, sheltered behind boxes and screened with handkerchiefs.

Thus, crouching together in the dark, they pressed close against each other. Leo remembered experiencing a special feeling of love for his brothers in playing that game. But, though the Ant-brotherhood was thus revealed to the children, the chief secret still remained hidden. They were never able to find the green stick on which was written the way for all men to cease suffering, leave off quarreling, and become continuously happy. Nevertheless, as Leo grew older, that was the secret he was ceaselessly striving to find, that he might disclose it to men.

Leo was only eight years old when the family moved to Moscow. They drove away from the old house, leaving behind them a crowd of staring, bare-footed children; menservants in coats and kaftans; and women in striped petticoats with babies in their arms.

Moscow was a very large and beautiful city, the Mother of all the Russias, for it was from little Mother Moscow that the whole great Russian empire had grown. The children admired the city greatly—its crooked old streets; its great open spaces and boulevards; the scores of white churches, each crowned with a dome of brilliant color, gold, green, or blue with silver stars. They loved to see the white palaces that overhung the narrow, winding banks of the Moskva River; the ancient monasteries with their high walls and round towers; and, best of all, the historic old fort of the Kremlin, sacred in Russian history. When they were not in school, they visited these places of interest; and, at such times, they rode in a carriage drawn by four bay horses harnessed abreast, according to the custom of the time and country.

They had only been a few months in Moscow, however, when their father suddenly died. And, as their mother was already dead, they were now total orphans with their Aunt Alexandra as their guardian. Count Nicolay disappeared so suddenly from Leo's life that the boy could not believe he was gone, but would scan the faces of passersby, thinking to see him again somewhere in the streets of Moscow.

For a time, the children lived with their grandmother, a very grand old lady who dwelt in considerable state and maintained the strictest etiquette in all the affairs of life.

But, soon after the death of Count Nicolay, Grandmother also died. Henceforth, the boys stayed in Moscow winters to go to school and went to Yasnaya Polyana for the summers. It was during those days that Leo learned for the first time that corporal punishment was being inflicted on the serfs at Yasnaya Polyana, a thing which had never been heard of when his father was alive. He and his brothers were returning from a walk with their tutor when they met near the barn the fat steward, Andrey Flyin. He was followed by the coachman's assistant, Squinting Koozma, as he was called. Koozma was a married man no longer young, and he wore just then a very piteous face. One of the children asked Andrey where he was going, and the steward quietly answered:

"We are going to the barn where Koozma must be punished."

This meant that Koozma was to be whipped, and it was a terrible feeling that came upon Leo at sight of the good-natured, crest-fallen fellow on the way to such a punishment. In the evening he told his Aunt Tatiana what had happened. She was moved to the heart and said to the boy: "And why did you not stop it?"

And why did he not stop it? He had not even dreamed before that he could interfere in such an affair. Could he stop it? He never forgot the incident.

In 1841, when Leo was thirteen years old, Aunt Alexandra died, and now the children fell to the care of another of their father's sisters, Aunt Pelageya, the wife of Yushkoff, a rich landowner of Kazan. Aunt Pelageya came almost at once and took her niece and nephews from Yasnaya Polyana to Kazan. Ordering some boats, she loaded them with everything which it was possible for her to take away from her brother's estate. All the servants had to follow her, too—carpenters, tailors, blacksmiths, chefs, upholsterers. Moreover, she gave to each of the four brothers a serf of about his own age, to be forever attached to him as a man-servant.

When all was ready, Leo and his sister and brothers bade farewell to their beloved Aunt Tatiana, who went to live with a sister, and set out in numerous carriages and other vehicles for Kazan. It was a long journey and they crept along very slowly, but the time of year was autumn, the weather was fine, and they often camped out in the fields, or the woods, bathing when they came to streams of water and feasting on fresh mushrooms. Thus they traveled for four hundred miles east of Moscow.

They found Kazan a half barbaric city, one of the most interesting in Russia. It was the busy gateway to the East, and from its quays they saw ships floating out on the mighty waters of the

river Volga, bound for the distant Caspian Sea. They saw its marts crowded with picturesque caravans, arriving from Bokhara and other cities of Persia, or departing perhaps for India, while its streets were thronged with Greeks, Tartars, Persians, dark-skinned Armenians and wayfarers from the Caucasus, a motley multitude indeed.

At the house of his uncle Yushkoff, in Kazan, Leo grew to manhood, and he and his brothers attended the university of Kazan. But it was altogether too gay a life he led there as a youth. Balls, now at the house of the governor of the province, now given by the chief of the nobility, private dancing parties, masquerades in the Hall of the Nobles, private theatricals, living-pictures, concerts all followed each other in an endless chain. As a titled young man of good birth, grandson of an ex-governor of Kazan, Tolstoy, in spite of his awkwardness and shyness, was welcomed everywhere.

Aunt Pelageya, a worldly minded woman, thought that the greatest happiness for Leo would be to marry a wealthy bride who would bring him an enormous number of serfs, and to become adjutant to the Czar. This was the highest ambition she held for him. The youth himself, however, was torn between two states of feeling. At times he enjoyed the dancing and card-playing and gambling as much as the most roisterous of his companions. At other times he despised it all, and bitterly reproached himself for wasting his time in such junketing. Then he longed to break away from that useless, shameful foolery and to do something more worth while.

In such a mood as this, he did at last break away from Kazan. He left the university where he never did overly well, and went back to Yasnaya Polyana, for the estate had fallen to him, when the property of his parents had been divided among the brothers.

Now the young man, who as a boy had been so intensely moved at seeing a serf on his way to be whipped, was fired with a great desire to take up farming seriously and to better the condition of his peasants. He wished to clean up their houses, to give them better implements to work with, to found schools and educate them. He even put on a workman's blouse and labored by their side. But he found his attempts to help the serfs received by them with suspicion and distrust. They preferred the filthy huts where they had lived so long to any new or better housing. Neatness and improved sanitary arrangements were a nuisance to them. They chose to keep their primitive old wooden sokha which only scratched the surface of the soil, rather than learn to use a modern iron plow. It was a strange sight for them to see their master working with them and they lost their respect for him. Neither did he succeed in arousing in them the slightest interest in education. Indeed, matters turned out so badly that his worldly-minded Aunt Pelageya was well able to say, "I told you so."

And so for a while young Tolstoy turned his back on the ideas for helping his people which had surged in him with such force. At this time his oldest brother, Nicolay, came home for a visit. Nicolay was with the Russian army in the wild mountain lands of the Caucasus, and when the day came for him to return to his duties, Leo left Yasnaya with all its wearisome problems and went off to seek adventure with him.

Years before, when the kingdom of Moscow became so strong as to make head against the Tartars, those barbarous half Mongol, half Turkish tribes that haunted its borderland, it gradually pushed them to the South East, and having conquered the kingdoms of Kazan and Astrakhan, it came into conflict with the wild tribes of Tartar mountaineers who inhabited the northern slopes of the Caucasian mountains. To keep these mountaineers in check, the Russian government had, about the middle of the nineteenth century, erected a whole line of palisaded forts as outposts. The Cossacks, who manned these forts were a warlike, pastoral people, particularly renowned as horsemen, and they furnished valuable contingents of cavalry to the Russian army. As time went on, the kingdom of Georgia on the southern slope of the mountains, became subject to Russia, and it was then absolutely necessary for Russia to subjugate those mountain tribes that separated her from her new domain. Thus the struggle went on for over fifty years, and it was to this scene of activity that Nicolay and Leo were bound.

The two young men traveled on horseback to Saratof, then in a fishing boat, rowing or drifting with the current, for a matter of three weeks down the river Volga till they came to Astrakhan on the Caspian Sea. From Astrakhan they journeyed in a post-chaise till they reached the Caucasus, and finally they came to the fortified camp of Stari Yurt. As they approached the place Leo suddenly saw a chain of snow-capped peaks rising directly from the flat prairie land of the steppes. The sun rose and glistened on the mountains and on the river Terek beyond the reeds. From a Cossack village came a native cart, and women, beautiful young women, walking. From that moment Leo understood the beauty and majesty of the mountains. From that moment everything he saw, everything he thought, everything he felt, assumed for him a new, severely majestic character, that of the mountains. All his Kazan memories with their shame and remorse vanished.

"Now life has begun," a solemn voice seemed to say to him.

At Stari Yurt, Nicolay and Leo lived in a tent. There were beautiful views about the place, in particular toward a spot where there were hot springs. There lay an enormous mountain of rocks all piled one upon another and intersected by torrents of boiling water, which in some places fell with much noise, and covered all the high part of the mountains with a steaming white vapor. In the middle of the valley, on the chief torrent, there were three water mills, one above the other, constructed in a peculiar and very picturesque way. All day the Tartar women

kept coming to wash their clothes above and below these mills. They washed them with their feet. To Leo, looking on, the whole scene seemed like an ant heap in continual motion. The women were for the most part handsome and well built, and notwithstanding their poverty, their oriental costumes were always graceful. The picturesque groups formed by the women, together with the savage beauty of the place, made a truly beautiful sight. Leo sometimes remained for hours admiring it all.

The manner of warfare in these wild outposts was barbarous. Cossack detachments attacked Tartar villages in the mountains, destroyed their pastures, drove off the cattle, captured as many inhabitants as possible and with such booty returned to the posts. The mountaineers made reprisals. They pursued the detachments on the way back, and with well-aimed carbine shots, inflicted great losses. They hid behind ramparts in the woods and narrow ravines, and sometimes even appeared suddenly at the very posts, where they massacred many and carried off men and women to the mountains.

Nicolay was an officer but for some time Leo remained merely a visitor and did not join the army. The wonderful beauty of the mountains, the wild Cossack and Tartar villages, the Cossack bravery, and the almost primitive simplicity of life, in sharp contrast with the stifling luxury of life in Moscow and Kazan, inspired him like a fresh clean wind blowing away an oppressive heat. He began to write, and sent back home for publication a novel called *Childhood*, for which he drew largely on his own memories of early days. But within a year, he, too, joined the army and took part in many a wild raid from which he more than once narrowly escaped with his life.

In 1853 Russia declared war against Turkey, and was fighting with great success both on land and sea, when France and England, fearing lest Russia should become too powerful, intervened against her and began what was called the Crimean War, which was marked by the long siege and heroic defence of Sebastopol, one of the most remarkable feats in history. At this time Leo got himself transferred from the Caucasus to the army of the Danube, which was bound for Sebastopol. He journeyed by sleigh the greater part of the way to Bucharest in Roumania, completing his journey in a wretched little cart, over terrible roads. On November 7, 1854, he reached Sebastopol. The spirit of the troops manning the batteries and the walls there, was beyond description.

"Such heroism," Leo wrote home to his aunt, "was never seen in ancient Greece." And he put his impressions of the whole in a series of Sebastopol sketches, which were published at home in Russia. But with the fall of Sebastopol and the close of the Crimean war, Leo had seen enough of fighting. He retired from the army and went home again to his beloved Yasnaya Polyana.

And now he fell to farming and the work of uplifting his serfs with a new and more serious enthusiasm. Though he traveled abroad a number of times, and lived occasionally in Moscow or Petrograd, his heart and soul were wholly in his work at Yasnaya Polyana,—his school there, his farming. He thought almost altogether of helping the people, of educating them. He dwelt continually on the real equality of man, and the terrible inequalities that human conditions presented. Often such things as these made him very miserable, but he forever persevered, seeking the real meaning of life, and the secret of how all men could be happy. Ah, could he but have found that little green stick which Nicolay had buried by the ravine so long ago!

Before he knew it, Leo was thirty-five years old, and very lonely, for he had no wife. And then one day he found that Sofiya Behrs, whom he had long known as a little girl, had suddenly grown to be a young lady. She was the daughter of Leo's first childish sweetheart, a little girl who lived near the Tolstoys and often came running in to surprise the family by masquerading at Yuletide. It took Leo but a very short time to realize that he wanted to marry Sofiya, and accordingly Yasnaya Polyana soon had a fair young mistress.

And now Leo thought that he could never again be unhappy. He loved Sofiya dearly. Children began to come, boys and girls, and they were a merry crowd. Leo played games and pranks with the merriest of them. His books, too, novels chiefly, were well received and his name was honored in Russia. And yet he could never wholly leave off thinking about the rich and the poor, neither could he save himself from being troubled at the injustice in human life, nor from trying to set it right.

When he grew too weary of himself and of the questions which were tormenting him, he would take his family and go for the summer to a great farm which he had bought at Samara, far off on the river Volga in the midst of the Russian steppes. That wide expanse of treeless prairie with its waving grasses has always had a great charm for the Russian, just as the desert has for the Arab. There Tolstoy had bought a herd of one hundred Bashkir mares, which he placed in charge of a Bashkir named Mahmud Shah. Mahmud came with his wife and set up his kotchovka, a conical tent made of felt stretched over a wooden frame and provided with a tiny painted door. This tent with its carpet and cushions and a beautifully decorated saddle hung up on one side, was so neat and luxurious, that Tolstoy called it the drawing room. When male visitors appeared, Mahmud's wife, not wishing to be seen of men, retired behind gay chintz curtains and handed out a wooden platter laden with glasses and bottles of kumys, the fermented mare's milk for which Samara was famous.

Tolstoy's herds increased rapidly though wandering Kirghiz tribesmen once made a raid on them and would have captured them all, had not a sturdy pair of Bashkir plowmen chased the robbers away.

When the family was at Samara they liked to live like Mahmud Shah in a Tartar kotchovka, and they watched with eager interest all the primitive methods of farming. There was the ploughing with five or six yokes of oxen, all wearing around their necks the deep-toned, melancholy bells; and when it came to threshing, there was a ring of horses tied head to tail, and kept circling round and round over the sheaves, while a Bashkir, armed with a long whip, acted as the ringmaster.

Once Tolstoy sent out an announcement that there would be races and other sports on his estate at Samara. The Bashkirs and Ural Cossacks, the well-to-do Russian peasants who lived in the neighboring villages and were very friendly with Tolstoy, all were invited. The prizes were to be an ox, a horse, a gun, a clock, a dressing-gown and other articles. A level place was selected for the races; a large circle five kilometers in circumference was marked with a plow, and starting posts were erected.

Soon the nomads began to arrive, bringing tents, copper boilers, sheep and gallons of kumys. Several thousand people assembled, and their tents were pitched on the steppe where the feather-grass waved in the breeze. The chief men among the Bashkirs took their positions on conical hillocks and sat cross-legged on their carpets, while a young Bashkir poured kumys from a leathern bottle and gravely handed the cup to each of the circle in turn. Here and there and everywhere was heard the weird minor music of the herdsmen's pipes and little snatches of song.

Then the games began,—wrestlers displayed their skill and for the principal races ten-year-old boys contended, mounted bareback on thirty finely-trained horses. No police were present, but, in spite of the clamor and excitement, good humor and order prevailed, and this particularly pleased Count Tolstoy. When the games were over, the guests were treated to horse-flesh and mutton and they departed satisfied, many of them politely thanking their host for his hospitality.

At this time the life of the Bashkir peasants, with all their flies, fleas and dirt, the wandering, nomadic life of millions of men scattered over an immense territory and struggling with primitive conditions, seemed to Tolstoy far more important than the political life of Europe as represented in the British parliament. And these years were the summit of his family happiness, his literary fame and wealth. The time was soon to come when even his splendid new domain of rich and fertile soil, with three hundred head of horses, could no longer satisfy him or restore him his inner peace.

The old questions came back with an insistence which made

it impossible to deny them. More and more he came to hate the idle, frivolous, useless life of the rich, the injustice of governments and society which gave so much to the rich and so little to the poor, the jealousies and selfishness that made war among men. He wanted to get back to the pure Christianity that Jesus taught, to lead a life of simplicity and work, of love and brotherhood. He wanted to love all, rich and poor, Zulu and idiot alike, and never be angry with anyone. He wanted to see all men equal, working and sharing alike. And so he lived among his peasants at Yasnaya Polyana, sharing with them the hardest manual labor and dressing just as they did, a smock in summer, a sheepskin coat and cap in winter.

And now instead of going on writing novels like those which had made him famous, he turned all his thoughts to religion and education. How to educate the peasants? How to teach them what was really good and fine? How to write for them so they would understand? These thoughts absorbed him.

Gradually he came to believe that owning property was wrong. He decided that men should hold all things in common, and he made over everything he possessed to his wife and children. He gave up the use of his title of Count, and he taught that men should not resist evil with violence nor go to war for any cause whatever. These ideas of his began to spread like wildfire among the masses who looked upon him as a deliverer, and to Yasnaya Polyana came many a pilgrim wishing to study his teachings. Nevertheless, the Greek Church and the Russian government frowned darkly on his views. Policemen raided his home and carried off writings regarded by them as seditious, while the church cast him out altogether.

Still the old man pursued his course to the end. More than once he tried to leave home in order to be absolutely free from the comforts in which his wife and children lived and on a plane of complete equality with the poorest among the peasants. Every

time, however, he returned. Not until a few days before his death, when he was eighty-two years old, did he leave Yasnaya Polyana for the last time, never to return.

On a gray, gloomy morning long before light, he set out, as eager to escape into poverty as most men would be to run off and seek a fortune. Sometimes he traveled in a dirty, ill-ventilated third-class car attached to a freight train, and filled with a crowd of evil-smelling workmen. Again he rode through a pouring rain. But at last on this strange and lonely journey, away from all his family save one daughter who had joined him, he was taken ill, and he died in the humble little old red house of a village station master.

Thither the peasants came in their long overcoats to stand in groups around the doorstep, weeping and embracing one another, and one was heard to comfort the others, saying:

"Fear not for him; he loved the people so."

Old man though he lived to be, Tolstoy never forgot the game of ant-brothers which he had played as a child, and when he was over seventy, he wrote:

"The ideal of 'ant-brothers,' lovingly clinging to one another, though not under two arm chairs curtained by handkerchiefs, but of all mankind under the wide dome of heaven, has remained the same for me. As I then believed that there existed a little green stick, whereon was written the message that could destroy all evil in men and give them universal welfare, so I now believe that such truth exists and will be revealed to men and will give them all it promises."

Stories for Children   Childhood   Gospel Stories   Twenty-three Tales

HALLS OF FAME

The Ugly Duckling

HANS CHRISTIAN ANDERSEN (*Danish*, 1805-1875)

It matters not to have been born in a duck-yard if one has been hatched from a swan's egg.

A HUNDRED years or more ago there lived in the ancient city of Odense in Denmark, an awkward, overgrown, lean little boy, as lanky and ungainly as any ugly duckling. Hans Andersen's father was a cobbler, his mother a washerwoman, and they were so poor that they lived in one room under a steep gabled roof. This room had to be kitchen and parlor, workshop and bedroom all in one, but, poor as it was, it seemed to Hans wonderfully exciting. In every corner it was full of interesting things. The walls were covered with pictures; the tables and chests had shiny cups, glasses and jugs upon them; in the lattice window grew pots of mint; from the rafters hung bunches of sweet herbs, and there were always fresh green boughs hanging here and there about. Over by the window, where the sun streamed in, was a cobbler's work-bench and a shelf of books. But most interesting of all to Hans was the door of the room which was brightly painted with pictures. Often when the little fellow had gone to bed and his mother and father thought him fast asleep, he would lie awake to look at those pictures and make up stories about them. In the day time he liked to crawl up the ladder and out on the roof of the house, where, in the gutter between the Andersen's cottage and the one next door, there stood a box of earth in which Hans's mother had planted chives and parsley. This was their garden, for all the world like Kay and Gerda's garden in *The Snow Queen*.

Hans's father, though he passed his days pounding pegs into shoes, was a very well educated man, who had seen far better

days. He loved to read, and spent all his spare time with books. This made him seem very different from his poor neighbors and even from his wife who had no education at all. He and Hans were great friends and they often went on long rambles into the woods together. While the father sat and thought, or read, Hans ran about and gathered wild strawberries or made pretty garlands of flowers. Aye, the boy liked well enough to go tramping with his father, he even liked to read as his father did, but when it came to learning lessons, that was a different matter. He had no more wish to do sums than a butterfly or a bird.

As a child he would play all alone out in the tiny garden behind the house. For hours he would sit near their one gooseberry bush, where, with the help of a broomstick and his mother's apron, he had made a little tent. Under this shelter he would sit cozily in all kinds of weather, fancying things and inventing stories. His father had made him some wonderful toys, pictures that changed their shape when pulled with a string, a mill which made the miller dance when it turned around, and a peep show of odd rag dolls. Hans liked best of all to play with this little toy theatre, for he was unusually fond of plays. He would dress up these little rag puppets and very seriously make them go through the actions of many a thrilling drama.

Occasionally, though very seldom, the boy went to school.

Once he made friends at school with a little girl, to whom he told many remarkable stories. These stories were chiefly about himself, and his favorite one was how he was really of noble birth and not the son of the cobbler at all, only the fairies had changed him in his cradle and nobody knew the truth about him! One day he heard the little girl say, "Hans is a fool." Poor little Hans! He trembled and told her no more stories.

When Hans was only eleven years old his father died and he was left alone with his mother. He still continued to play with his toy theatre, but now it was reading, which, more than anything else, absorbed him and he read every book on which he could lay his hands. Best of all he loved Shakespeare. He liked particularly those plays where there were ghosts or witches. Indeed, he became so devotedly fond of the drama that he felt he must be an actor. He could sing well, too, he decided.

One day an old woman who was washing clothes in the river told Hans that the Empire of China lay down there under the water. Having taken no pains to learn anything about the world, Hans quite believed her and thought to himself that perhaps, on a moonlight night when he should be singing down by the water's edge, a Chinese prince, charmed by his marvelous music, would push his way up through the earth and take him down to China to make him rich and noble. Then the prince might let him return some day to Odense, where he would build a castle, to be envied and admired by all who had once despised him!

Naturally enough, young Hans singing in the lanes, reading and playing theatre alone by himself at home, was despised and looked upon almost as a lunatic by the people of Odense. Tall, gawky boy that he was, he had a huge nose, tiny eyes and a long, lanky neck like a bird's. His feet and hands were as big as boats, and his clothes were always too small. Ah, he was the laughing stock of the neighborhood! Boys teased him and screamed after him, "There goes the play scribbler."

Wounded to the quick, Hans shrank away from them all and hid himself at home, to be safe from their mockery. He had not a single friend of his own age in Odense.

The gentry who lived round about, though they were amused by the cobbler's peculiar son, were also sorry for him. They laughed at his absurd ambitions to be a great writer, a singer or an actor, when he had never taken the trouble to get even the smallest education, but they tried, also, to induce him to go to school. For a time he did as they wished, but in school he was always dreamy and absent-minded, and he never bothered to study. Indeed, he tried to please his master by bringing him wild flowers instead of learning his lessons.

At length, at the age of fourteen, Hans came to the conclusion that, like the heroes he had read about in his books, he must set out into the world and seek his fortune. This meant that he would go to Copenhagen and find work at the theatre. He had heard of a wonderful thing called a ballet which seemed to him grander and finer than anything else in the world, and his head was full of a certain marvelous lady who danced in that ballet. Hans pictured this chief dancer as a sort of fairy queen, who should graciously condescend to help him and, by a single wave of her hand, make him famous.

Now Fru Andersen was rather alarmed at these plans of her son's; so she sought advice from a fortune-teller. That wise woman consulted the coffee grounds and solemnly announced that

Hans Christian Andersen would be a very great man. One day all Odense should be illumined to do him honor! This statement seemed ridiculous, too utterly ridiculous. It was received with many a wink and shrug of the shoulders by knowing friends of the family, but it satisfied Hans's mother and she consented to let him go. So the boy confidently did up his little bundle, and with nine dollars in his pocket, took ship for Copenhagen.

Once arrived in the city, he hurried away to find his fairy queen, the chief dancer of the ballet, and he poured out in her wondering ears his longing to go on the stage. To show her what he could do, he took off his shoes and began dancing about in his stocking feet, using his hat for a drum and beating a lively tattoo! Needless to say, the graceful gambols of this overgrown giraffe terrified the poor lady. She took him for a lunatic and hastily showed him the door.

In spite of his disappointment, Hans persisted. He went to seek help from the Director of the Theatre, but it was only to meet with another rebuff. "None but educated men," said the director, "are engaged to go on the stage."

And so began the long series of Hans's adventures and disappointments. Ridiculous as he appeared to others, he respected himself sincerely and never lost his firm belief in his own ability. Some day something wonderful would happen to him surely! But he was keenly sensitive, too, and the constant rebuffs he met with always hurt him sorely. All the unhappiness of those days, as well as of his childhood, he expressed years later in the story of the Ugly Duckling, whose buffetings and miseries represent his own early trials.

He lived now in a garret in the poorest quarter of Copenhagen, and had nothing to eat but a cup of coffee in the morning and a roll later on in the day. True, he found friends who recognized his talent and wished to help him, but he was too proud to take from them more than was absolutely necessary. He would

pretend that he had had plenty to eat and that he had been dining out with friends, rather than accept their charity. He would say, too, that he was quite warm when his clothes were threadbare and his boots so worn and leaky that his feet were sopping with water. The courage and determination he showed at this time were really remarkable in a lad only fifteen years old. Once he sent a play which he had written to the Royal Theatre, never doubting in his childish ignorance but that it would be accepted. Here should begin his grand and glorious fortunes! Here all his dreams should begin to come true. Alack! the play came back to him all too soon with the curt comment that it showed such a lack of education as to be absolutely absurd. Here was a blow indeed, a hard blow to the boy's high hopes. But he would not be put down. Nothing daunted, he swallowed his disappointment once again, and wrote another play. This time those who read his manuscript at the theatre were surprised to discover that it showed unmistakable signs of talent, and they advised Andersen's friends to ask the King for money to send the boy to school.

Frederick VI of Denmark was like the kind kings in Andersen's stories. He arranged at once that Hans should be sent to school, and from then on he helped the boy until he was able to care for himself. Hans was not happy in school, however. There he was, a great hulking lad of seventeen, having to go into classes with the very smallest boys. He had plenty of opportunity now to wish that he had applied himself in earlier days to his lessons.

But though he worked hard, both here and later at the University in Copenhagen, he found it difficult to learn, and was generally thought a dunce. He continued to write poems, plays and sketches, which were one and all pronounced wishy-washy and silly. He failed again and again. Yet in the very bottom of his heart, in spite of all his failures, something always said, "I can," and his faith in himself never faltered.

At length, Frederick VI allowed him money for foreign travel, and he set forth to visit Italy, Germany and France. In Italy, among the ruins of old Rome that dot the Campagna, he found his inspiration for his first successful novel, *The Improvisatore,* which was published on his return to Copenhagen.

During all this time Andersen had been looking solely to his novels and plays to win him recognition. But while he was doing work of the most ordinary merit in this line, he had one admirable talent which he never even dreamed of taking seriously. Odense, his birthplace, was a rich treasure house of legends and folk lore, and sometimes, just to amuse the children of his friends, he would gather the little ones about him and weave these old legends into the most wonderful of stories. He would tell these tales in the liveliest manner, never bothering about grammar, but using childish words, and as he talked he would act and jump about and make remarkable faces. The children were delighted.

Perceiving all this, Andersen's friends at length suggested to him that he should write down these stories to make a book. At first he laughed at such an idea, but finally, more in fun than in earnest, he consented to the plan and wrote the stories down exactly as he had told them. This made them different from anything else that had ever been published in Denmark. Most people, when they write, have a formal, stilted manner, quite different from their ordinary conversation, but Andersen's tales were written in the same lively, simple, informal style in which he had told them. In this lay their peculiar charm. The critics, of course—that is, those who were not too grand even to look at such childish trash—criticized the stories for this informal style and bewailed the lack of elegance in their wording. Even Andersen himself did not take these "small things" seriously. Little did he dream that it was to be his fairy tales and nothing else which should win him his lasting fame. In them he gave free rein to his wonderful fancy. In them he embodied all the childlike simplicity of his great and loving heart. Soon the stories became so popular that they were translated into one foreign language after another, and while Andersen's novels and plays have long since been forgotten, it is due to his fairy tales that he is still known and loved throughout the world.

The recognition thus won by Andersen after so many years of struggle was, to him, a source of constant wonder and delight. That he, the son of a poor washerwoman and a cobbler, should now be the friend of princes and kings, seemed to him more marvelous than any story of Cinderella. Often when he was enjoying some quite ordinary luxury which most people take for granted, such as lying on a sofa in a new dressing gown, surrounded by books, he would think of his childhood and wonder. On his travels, too, he found himself welcomed everywhere on the friendliest terms by the greatest men in the literature of his day. Now, when he passed along the streets of Copenhagen, those who caught sight of him would cry, "There goes the great poet!" Quite different from the days when the boys had shrieked after him, "There goes the play scribbler!"

On December sixth, 1867, when Andersen was sixty-two years old, the prophecy made so long ago to his mother was fulfilled. In Odense, the city of his birth, the once scorned and ugly little boy was greeted with an immense celebration. To do him honor, all the town, from end to end, was one great blaze of light. And so, at last, the ugly duckling turned out, in truth, to be a swan.

ANDERSEN'S FAIRY TALES THE IMPROVISATORE

The Interesting History of Old Mother Goose

THE most remarkable dame in all history who was born gray-headed and yet never grows old, who perennially keeps her charm, who is ever, forever, calling out the spirit of childhood in the human heart to go gamboling with her over the green, turning somersaults, kicking up its heels, and yet learning, too, at her knee from her quaint store of sage and precious nonsense, is that beloved old creature, Old Mother Goose. Who she was, nobody knows. Her personality remains enshrouded in the most delightful mystery. But, if the truth were known, she has doubtless dwelt forever in the human heart; for her rhymes and jingles are nothing more nor less than the spontaneous bubblings of the eternal spirit of childhood, that delicious, joyous, nonsensical wisdom which is foolishness only to men.

The rhymes and jingles of Old Mother Goose are a gradual growth like the folk tales, composed at no one time by no one individual, but springing up all down through the ages, who knows how?—naturally, spontaneously, joyously, like the droll little Jack-in-the-Pulpits and Dutchmen's-Breeches of the woodland. They need no other claim to a reason for being than the pure joy of expressing that bubbling spirit (albeit sometimes by means of well nigh meaningless words) and the everlasting delight of man in rhyme and rhythm and musical arrangement of sounds. What other excuse for existence, save its beautiful arrangement of s's, is needed by that immortal line—"Sing a Song of Sixpence!"

There have been many interesting theories as to the origin of the name Mother Goose. But the one most stoutly maintained was advanced in the quaint little volume published at Boston in the year 1833 by the firm of Munroe and Frances, under the title, *The Only True Mother Goose, without addition or abridgment, embracing also a reliable Life of the Goose Family never before published.*

According to this story a certain Thomas Fleet, born in England and brought up in a printing office in the city of Bristol, came to Boston in the year 1712 when that city was little more than an over-grown village with its narrow, crooked streets still bespeaking the cow-paths from which they sprang. Here Thomas Fleet established a printing office in that street of the delectable name, Pudding Lane, where he published small books, pamphlets and such matter as came to hand. It was not long before he became acquainted with a well-to-do family of the name of Goose, and he grew exceedingly fond of the pretty young daughter, Elizabeth Goose. Under the date June 8, 1715, there appears in the record of marriages still preserved in the historic old town hall of Boston, an entry recording the wedding by the famous Reverend Cotton Mather, of Thomas Fleet, "now residing in Pudding Lane of this city, to Elizabeth Goose."

The happy couple took up their residence in the same quaint little house with the small paned windows where the printing office was situated in Pudding Lane, and Elizabeth's mother, Old Mother Goose, went to live with them. Here various children were born to the Fleets, and Old Mother Goose, being a most devoted grandmother, was so over-joyed that she spent the greater part of her time in the nursery, pouring out to the little ones the songs and ditties which she had learned in her childhood.

The industrious father Fleet, having these ditties constantly dinned into his ears, shrewdly conceived the idea of collecting the songs and publishing them. This he did under the title, *Songs for the Nursery or Mother Goose's Melodies*, and he sold the same from the Pudding Lane shop for the price of two coppers apiece. The story further goes on to relate how a goose with a very long neck and a wide open mouth flew across the title page of the book; and Munroe and Frances solemnly announced that they had merely reprinted these wonderful original verses.

This interesting, picturesque, and delightful tale may or may not be true. Certainly the grave of Old Mother Goose remains to this very day carefully marked in one of Boston's old churchyards, where it is visited by many devoted pilgrims each year; but unfortunately, no scrap of the original book has ever been found to corroborate the claim of Messrs. Munroe and Frances. Moreover, whether the tale be true or not, it still in no way explains the origin of the name Mother Goose; for in the very childhood of Thomas Fleet, more than twenty years before his supposed publication of *Mother Goose's Melodies*, there appeared in France a little prose collection of the best known fairy tales, *Cinderella, Little Red Riding Hood, Toads and Diamonds, Bluebeard, Sleeping Beauty*, etc. These were written by a most distinguished French writer, Charles Perrault, were published in Paris in the year 1697, and were called *Contes de ma Mère, l'Oye*, or, *Tales of My Mother, the Goose*. On the frontispiece of his book is an old woman spinning and telling tales to a man, a girl, a boy, and a cat. It is not even known whether Perrault originated the name Mother Goose, for it is said, that long before his time, the goose had been given the reputation for story telling. Instead of saying of stories the origin of which they did not care to disclose, "A little bird told me!" people used to say, "Oh, a goose told me!" And so, after all, perhaps even the name Mother Goose belongs to the people and not to any one individual.

These tales of Perrault's, however, were all in prose while it is through her rhymes and jingles that Mother Goose has won her best-deserved fame. The first known collection of rhymes under her name was published in London about 1765, having been gathered together by John Newbery, the famous publisher of St. Paul's Churchyard, and the first publisher in the world to give special attention to children's books. It was he who published *Little Goody Two Shoes*, the story generally attributed to that prime friend of childhood, Oliver Goldsmith, who undoubtedly edited the *Mother Goose Melodies* for Newbery. In Welsh's *Life of Goldsmith* we are told that Goldsmith taught a certain little maid "Jack and Jill by two bits of paper on his fingers," and that after the successful production of his play *The Good-natured Man*, Mr. Goldsmith was so overjoyed that he sang lustily for his friends his favorite song, "about an old woman tossed in a blanket seventeen times as high as the moon."

In 1785 Newbery's edition of Mother Goose was reprinted in Worcester, Massachusetts, by Isaiah Thomas, who had married one of the grand-daughters of Thomas Fleet, and a great-grand-daughter of old Dame Goose. A very beautiful copy of this book is to be found in the Boston Library, and since the story of Thomas Fleet's edition cannot be proved, John Newbery must be accepted as the first publisher, and Isaiah Thomas as the first American publisher, of our best beloved nursery classic.

Some twenty years after the Thomas edition, another collection of nursery rhymes appeared, called *Gammer Gurton's Garland*, which contained all of the *Mother Goose Melodies* and a great many more besides, but much of this material was taken from old jest books, and was worthless and coarse, and *Gammer Gurton's Garland* never attained the popularity of Mother Goose.

In 1842, James Halliwell, a man of fine scholarship, made a careful study of the nursery rhymes of England, collected principally from oral tradition. He writes that these nonsense scraps "have come down in England to us in such numbers that in the short space of three years the author has collected considerably more than a thousand." Besides Halliwell, many other men of the highest literary ability have edited Mother Goose.

It is intensely interesting to know how very old some of our best known rhymes are. In the preface to the Newbery edition, the writer, probably Oliver Goldsmith, says, "The custom of singing these songs and lullabies to children is of very great antiquity. It is even as old as the time of the ancient Druids. Charactacus, King of the Britons, was rocked in his cradle in the Isle of Mona, now called Anglesea, and tuned to sleep by some of these soporiferous sonnets." Old King Cole was certainly an ancient Celtic king of about the third century A. D., an original Briton, who lived even before the Angles and Saxons had come to conquer England. Dim and far away seem those days in the dawn of English history when the Druids still held sway with the dark mysteries of their religion in the dusky oak forests of England, but the whole flashes suddenly into light and life when we realize that those were the very days when

Old King Cole
Was a merry old soul
And a merry old soul was he;
Old King Cole
He sat in his hole,
And called for his fiddlers three.
And every fiddler, he had a fine fiddle,
And a very fine fiddle had he,
"Tweedledee, tweedledee," said the fiddlers three.

Little Jack Horner, too, is probably early Celtic and was originally a long poem, containing the *Pleasant History of all Jack Horner's Witty Pranks*, of which the sticking of his thumb in the Christmas pie formed only an insignificant part.

Mother, May I Go Out to Swim? is fourteen hundred years old and comes from a jest book of the sixth century. Only to think that at the same time when minstrels were singing with wondrous dignity to courtly listeners in the great halls of the castles, the sonorous and heroic lines of the Beowulf, children in the nursery were snickering and giggling, just as we do today, over the ridiculous jingle,

Mother, may I go out to swim?
Yes, my darling daughter,
Hang your clothes on a hickory limb,
But don't go near the water!

And for every man of the present time who knows the classic Beowulf, there are at least five hundred who know the jingle!

I Had a Little Husband No Bigger Than My Thumb is probably a part of Tom Thumb's History and is supposed to have originated in the tenth century from a little Danish work treating of "Swain Tomling, a man no bigger than a thumb, who would be married to a woman three ells and three quarters long."

Humpty Dumpty dates back to the days of King John in the thirteenth century. When that tyrannical gentleman was quarreling with his barons and they were forcing him to grant them the Great Charter of England, Humpty Dumpty had already begun his immortal escapade of falling off the wall, and if one were to inquire which had won the more enduring fame by his exploits, the answer would necessarily be, that granting the foundation for all the liberties of England, could never place King John in the same rank with that prime entertainer of infancy, who will apparently be performing his antics unto all generations.

The rhyme of the old woman who was tossed up in a blanket

to sweep the cobwebs out of the sky was old in the days of Henry V, in the early fifteenth century. When that strong-handed monarch set out with a mere handful of men to conquer France, the faction opposed to him in his own country, used to sing the rhyme to ridicule him and show the folly and impossibility of his undertaking, representing the King as an old woman engaged in a pursuit the most absurd and extravagant possible. But when King Henry routed the whole French army at Agincourt, taking their king and the flower of their nobility prisoners, and made himself master of France in spite of his mere handful of men, the very people who had ridiculed him began to change their minds and think no task too difficult for him. They therefore cancelled the former sonnet and sang this one:

So vast is the prowess of Harry the Great,
He'll pluck a hair from the pale faced moon;
Or a lion familiarly take by the tooth,
And lead him about as you lead a baboon.
All princes and potentates under the sun,
Through fear into corners and holes away run;
While no danger nor dread his swift progress retards
For he deals with kingdoms as we do our cards!

The Queen whom Pussy Cat, Pussy Cat, made the famous expedition to London to see, appears to have been Queen Elizabeth, though why Pussy Cat, Pussy Cat reported nothing more interesting at court than frightening a little mouse under a chair, when she might have held forth on the subject of Queen Elizabeth in all the glory of her satins, and jewels, and stomachers, and puffs, and ruffs, and coifs, remains a secret known only to Pussy.

Simple Simon comes from a chapbook of the Elizabethan era. These chapbooks, which have furnished us with a number of our old rhymes, were small volumes filled with jokes and crude illustrations and carried about from place to place for sale by wandering peddlers or chapmen, who caught the attention of the common folk by means of a song or a jig, and then sold them not only treasures of literature but buttons, and pins and jewelry besides.

Sing a Song of Sixpence was well known in Shakespeare's time.

The unfortunate Hector Protector who was dressed all in green and met with such disfavor at the hands of the King as well as the Queen, was that doughty old Puritan, Oliver Cromwell, Lord High Protector of England, familiarly called Old Noll, who ousted Charles I from his throne and could scarcely be expected, henceforth, to be any too graciously dealt with by kings and queens.

From all this account which might be lengthened still further, it appears that Mother Goose is no mere modern upstart, but belongs to the pedigreed aristocracy of literature, and in spite of a few unworthy pranks which she has perpetrated in the form of coarse and vulgar rhymes, she must be treated with the respect which is due to so worthy and lovable an old dame.

The end

H A L L S   O F   F A M E

The World's Great Epics

AN EPIC is an heroic narrative, sometimes in prose, but most often in poetry, treating in heroic style a theme of heroic proportions. Its unity generally consists in the fact that all the incidents are grouped about one central hero. These stories were told and sung by wandering bards in hall and castle from generation to generation, until at last some poet appeared, of sufficient genius to write down the tale and give it permanent form in the peculiar style and rhythm of his own country.

THE greatest of all the world's epics, the *Iliad** and *Odyssey**—are attributed to Homer, who is said to have lived between 1050 and 850 B. C. For centuries they were publicly recited in the stately marble porticoes of Greek dwellings or on the dappled lawns of temple groves overlooking the blue Aegean. The *Iliad* or *Achilliad* relates the story of the Trojan War, and centers about the hero, Achilles. The *Odyssey* is the tale of the wanderings of Ulysses, or Odysseus, after the fall of Troy. Very like the Greek epics is the *Aeneid* of Virgil, the story of the wanderings of the Trojan, Aeneas.

*The Adventures of Odysseus *by Padraic Colum.* The Iliad for Boys and Girls *by A. J. Church.*
The Odyssey for Boys and Girls *by A. J. Church.* The Aeneid for Boys and Girls *by A. J. Church.*

Next in antiquity to the Greek epics is the Persian epic, *Shah-Nameh**, or Book of Kings, of which Rustem is a hero. This book was composed by the poet Abul Kasim Mansur about 920 A. D. Abul Kasim sang so sweetly that his master, the Shah, termed him Firdusi, or Singer of Paradise.

*The Story of Rustem *by Renninger.*

Following the Persian we have the two great East Indian sacred epics, the *Mahabharata** and the *Ramayana.** The *Ramayana* was composed in Sanscrit some five hundred years before Christ,

and is a strange mixture of the wildest and most preposterous legends with the truest and deepest philosophy. The poem is generally attributed to Valmiki, a hermit who dwelt on the bank of the Ganges. One day it chanced that Valmiki saw one bird of a happy pair slain, and he made use of so strange and expressive a meter in singing the pity stirred in his heart at the sight, that the god Brahma, the one supreme God of the Hindus, immediately bade him employ the same meter in narrating the adventures of Rama, who is supposed to be one of the seven appearances in the flesh of the god Vishnu, the preserver of men.

*THE INDIAN STORY BOOK *(Tales from the Ramayana and Maha-Bharata) by Richard Wilson.*

THE oldest epic in Europe is the Finnish* *Kalevala, Land of Heroes.* Although the *Kalevala* was not written down until the first half of the nineteenth century, when Topelius and Lönnrot painstakingly took it from the mouths of the people, it incorporates within it poems that doubtless date back some three thousand years into Finnish antiquity. The *Kalevala* relates the ever varying contests between the Finns and Laplanders, Light and Darkness, Good and Evil, the Finns signifying Light and Good, the Laplanders Darkness and Evil. The chief beauty of the poem is its wonderful rhythm and its splendid flights of imagination.

The poet who sang the song somewhere in the dim past says,

"Nature was my only teacher,
Woods and waters my instructors,"

and certainly, the rhythm of the poem does ring and trip and ripple with the very spirit of winds and waves and woodlands. Longfellow copied the strange rhythm of *Kalevala,* its alliterative use of words and its delightful repetitions, very perfectly in *Hiawatha.*

*THE SAMPO, *Hero Tales from the Finnish Kalevala, by James Baldwin.*

The best known of the Norse epics is the *Volsunga Saga**, the tale of Sigurd and Sigmund, descendants of Volsunga. It tells the famous story of how Sigurd slew the dragon, Fafnir, and how he broke through the ring of fire to rescue Brynhild, the Valkyr, from her long doom of sleep. The *Nibelungenlied*, the German story of the accursed golden hoard of the Nibelungs or dwarfs, was taken from the *Volsunga Saga*. A more beautiful Norse epic is the *Saga of Frithjof*.

*SIEGFRIED, THE HERO OF THE NORTH *by Ragozin.* THE STORY OF SIEGFRIED *by James Baldwin.* SIGURD THE VOLSUNG *by Morris.* FRITHJOF, THE VIKING OF NORWAY *by Ragozin.*

IN ENGLISH the *Beowulf* is our oldest epic. It was doubtless composed before the Angles and Saxons left Europe and settled in Britain. Among the Angles and Saxons the art of poetry was very generally cultivated and the harp was passed around at feasts that every guest might play and sing. Besides this, there were professional poets called in Old English, "scops or gleomen," who either travelled from place to place, or held permanent positions at the courts of chieftains or kings. These poets set out to sing of real events, but gradually they magnified the deeds of which they sang, and as the true event on which the poem was founded, receded into the past, the hero came to be pictured as enormously greater and stronger than he actually was, his deeds as infinitely more wonderful, until he became a sort of demi-god. Beowulf is held to have been a real person thus magnified, and stories about him arose among the Angles and Saxons in Europe in the seventh century A. D. These poems were originally heathen, which accounts for the mingling of heathen and Christian elements in the epic as we have it, for it was brought by the Anglo-Saxons to England, gradually transformed as they be-

came Christian, and written down at last by some Northumberland monk.

Though the scene of the poem is not England, the social conditions it depicts, the style in which it is written, and the virtues which it exalts, are thoroughly English.

Like all Old English poetry, *Beowulf* is not in meter. The characteristic of Old English verse was a line divided in the middle by a pause and marked by alliteration, two words in the first half of the line beginning with the same letter as one word at least in the second half of the line, as for example: "How deeds of daring were done by their athelings." Another interesting characteristic of Old English verse is the use of a phrase to imply a thing instead of the direct name for the thing, as, for example, calling the sea the whale-path or swan-road, and the sword the battle-friend, which makes for a lively descriptive style and lends an interesting variety to the whole.

Next in the story of the English epic is the Arthurian Cycle, a number of epics or romances about King Arthur and the knights of the Round Table. Arthur was probably a noble Celtic King of Britain in the early days of the Saxon invasion, but his original character was gradually transformed by story-tellers until, by the end of the twelfth century, he had become merely an ideal king by means of whom chivalry could express its highest aims and ideals. The best known English version of these tales was by Thomas Mallory and was written in prose. Tennyson's *Idylls of the King* are the Arthurian legends still further idealized and put into poetry.

The beloved Robin Hood story was compiled from some two score old English ballads, some going as far back as the year 1400, and all full of the Englishman's love for merry humor.

THE BOY'S KING ARTHUR *by Sidney Lanier.* THE MERRY ADVENTURES OF ROBIN HOOD *by Howard Plye.*
NORTHLAND HEROES (BEOWULF AND FRITHJOF) *by Florence Holbrook.*
UNA AND THE RED CROSS KNIGHT *by Royde Smith.*

In Ireland there were three great cycles of poetry sung by the old Gaelic bards long years ago when Ireland was still pagan and had her own Irish gods. These cycles consisted of scattered poems never put into one great whole, and the finest and most Irish of them all is the one dealing with Cuculain or Cuchulain and the Knights of the Red Branch. Cuculain and his friends are historical characters, seen as it were, through mists of love and wonder. The large manner of this antique Gaelic literature wipes out all littleness in its presence. Nothing small in the heart of man can stand before real sympathy with the enormous simplicity of this heroic tale of primitive Irish life.

THE CUCHULAIN *by Standish O'Grady.* THE BOY'S CUCHULAIN *by Eleanor Hull.*

The national epic in France bears the characteristic name, *Chanson de Geste,* or *Song of Deeds,* because the *trouvères* and the troubadours wandered from castle to castle singing the deeds of their lords. The greatest cycle of these chansons, of which there were three, dealt with Charlemagne, the champion of Christianity, and his twelve faithful paladins or peers.

THE STORY OF ROLAND *by James Baldwin.* FRITHJOF AND ROLAND *by Ragozin.*

In Spain the great epic poem is the *Cid,* written about 1200 A. D., a compilation from ballads already in existence. Rodrigo Diaz de Bivar, the Cid, was born about 1030 A. D. and his heroic deeds were performed at a time when Christian kings were making special efforts to eject the Moors from Europe.

THE STORY OF THE CID *by Wilson.*

INDEX

ART

B

E

LITERATURE

SEE ALSO LANGUAGE

See also Folk Literature; Folk Tales

MUSIC

Stories and notes about musical composition and musicians. These are arranged according to the period of music to which the composers belong.

DEVELOPMENT

N

Y

Z

Guide to the Pronunciation of Proper Names

THE DIACRITICAL MARKS USED ARE THE SAME AS GIVEN IN WEBSTER'S NEW INTERNATIONAL DICTIONARY

ā as in *ale*
ă as in *add*
ä as in *arm*
â as in *care*
ȧ as in *ask*
ȧ as in *chaotic*
ē as in *eve*
ĕ as in *end*
ẽ as in *maker*
ê as in *event*
ī as in *ice*
ĭ as in *ill*
ō as in *old*
ŏ as in *odd*
ȯ as in *obey*
ô as in *orb*
o͞o as in *food*
o͝o as in *foot*
ū as in *cube*
ŭ as in *up*
û as in *urn*
ů as in *unite*

Ariel, *âr'ĭ ĕl*
Aristophanes, *ăr'ĭs tŏf'ȧ nēz*
Aruman, *är ū'măn*
Asbjörnsen, *äs byûrn'sĕn*
Avon, *ā'vŭn*
Bali, *bä'lē*
Basel, *bā'zĕl*
Baudricourt, *bō'drē ko͞or*
Bellini, *bĕl lē'nē*
Berlioz, *bĕr'lē ōs'*
Björnson, Björnstjerne, *byûrn'-sŭn, byûrn shẽr'nĕ*
Boggin, *bŏg'ĭn*
Cammaerts (*kä'märts*), Émile
Campania, *käm pän'yä*
Cather, *kăth'ẽr*
Cawein, *kā wīn'*
Celtic, *sĕl'tĭk*
Chaucer, *chô'sẽr*
Cheyenne, *shī ĕn'*
Chopin, *shō'păn'*
Cinque Ports, *sĭngk pōrts*
Compiègné, *kôn'pyĕn'*
Czecho-Slovakia, *chĕk'ō-slō vä'kĭ ȧ*
Czechoslovakian, *chĕk'ō slō văk'ĭ-ăn*
Dagobert, *dăg'ō bẽrt* (*English*); *dȧ gō bâr'* (*French*)
Darius, *dȧ rī'ŭs*
Dasent, *dā'sĕnt*
Debeauve, *dĕ bō vā'*
Donuil Dhu, *dŏn'ĭl do͞o'*
Dovre, *dŏv'rĕ*
Dracul, *drā'ko͞ol*
Eloi, *ā'lwä*
Fabre, Henri, *fȧ'br', än'rē'*
Fernández, Juan, *fĕr nän' dāth* (*Spanish*); *fẽr năn' dēz* (*English*) *hwän'*
Fontaine, Jean de la, *fôn'tĕn', zhän dĕ lȧ*
Fra Angelico, *frä än jĕl'ē kō*
France, Anatole, *fräns, ăn'ȧ tōl*
Fröding, Gustaf, *frû'dĭng, gŭs tȧf'*
Galapagos, *gä lä'pä gōs*
Gallais, *găl'lā*
Gotham, *gŏth'ăm*
Grethel, *grā'tĕl*
Guillaume, *gē'yôm'*
Guiseppi, *gēz'ĕp pĭ*
Hiawatha, *hī ȧ wô'thȧ*
Hine Moa, *hē'nāy mō'ȧ*
Hjalmar, *yĕl'mär*
Hjuki, *yū'kē*
Hopi, *hō'pē*
Iduna, *ē do͞o'nȧ*
Jokeli, *yō'kĕ lĭ*
Jötunn-heim, *yō'to͞on-hām*
Leprechaun, *lĕp'rē kôn'*
Lombardy, *lŏm'bẽr dĭ*
Magna Charta, *măg'nȧ kär'tȧ*
Maoris, *mä'ō rĭz*
Mazurka, *mȧ zûr'kȧ*
Meleager, *mĕl'ē ā'jẽr*
Miller, Joaquin (*wȧ kēn'*)
Miller, Olive Beaupré (*bō prāy'*)
Mjolner, *myôl'nẽr*
Neapolitan, *nē'ȧ pŏl'ĭ tăn*
Nootka, *no͞ot'kä*
Odense, *ō'thĕn sȧ*
Peppino, *pāy pē'ē'nō*
Phaethon, *fā'ē ĭ'n*
Pharaoh, *fâ'rō; fā rō*
Phoebus Apollo, *fē'bŭs ȧ pŏl'ō*
Pierrot, *pē'ĕr ō*
Polonaise, *pō'lō nāz'*
Pombo, Rafael, *pŏm'bō, rä'fāy ĕl*
Poulsson, *pōl'sŭn*
Pueblo, *pwĕb'lō*
Rajah, *rä'jȧ*
Ramayana, *rä mä'yȧ nȧ*
Reinar, *rāy ē när'*
Restrepo, Don Antonio José, *res tra pō', dŏn ăn tō'nĭ ō hō sāy'*
Rhodopis, *rō dō'pĭs*
Shingebiss, *shĭn'ge bĭs*
Skrymir, *skĭr'mĭr*
Tagore, Rabindranath, *tȧ gōr', rȧ bĭn'drȧ nȧth*
Tchaikovsky, *chī kôf'skē*
Theognis, *thē ŏg'nĭs*
Thorne-Thomsen, Gudrun, *thôrn-tŏms'n, go͝od'ro͞on*
Titania, *tĭ tā'nĭ ȧ*
Tuscany, *tŭs'kȧ nĭ*
Tutaneikai, *to͞o'tȧ nā kāy*
Tyrol, *tĭr'ŏl*
Vancouleur, *văn ko͞o'lẽr*
Vecellio, Tiziano, *vȧ chĕl'lyō, tēt syä'nō*
Villon, François, *vē'yôn', frän swä'*
von Chamisso, *fôn shä'mĭ sō*
Zuñi, *zo͞o'nyē*

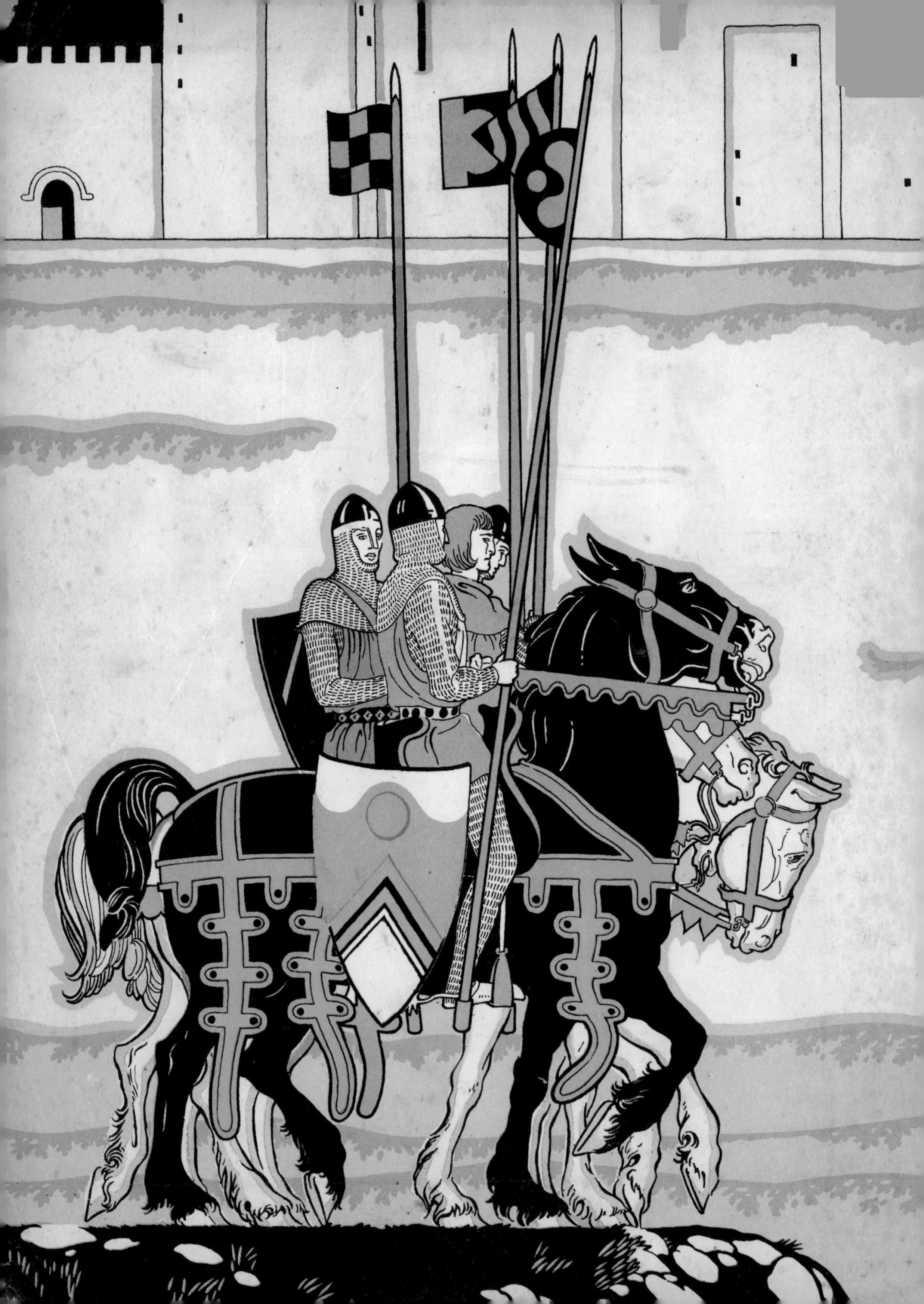